● **GROWTH MODELS FOR PROFESSIONAL LEADERS AND CONGREGATIONS**

CARING FOR THE CAREGIVER

AN ALBAN INSTITUTE PUBLICATION

GARY L. HARBAUGH

The Publications Program of The Alban Institute is assisted by a grant from Trinity Church, New York City.

Library of Congress Catalog Card Number 92-72793
ISBN 1-56699-059-9

CONTENTS

FOREWORD

Whenever we go out to buy a brand new automobile, we are bound to have an intense interest in the maintenance agreement. We want to know what the company will do for us while the car is under warranty; the fact is, no matter how well our cars are made, some are bound to break down before they reach 50,000 miles.

The same is true when buying an air conditioner or rototiller. Many of us wisely buy the maintenance agreement from the store so this equipment receives yearly maintenance.

Strange how we fail to think in similar terms as we launch men and women into the ordained ministry. Instead, our expectation is that these clergy will run non-stop, without a breakdown, until they retire. Whenever an ordained person does break down, either physically, emotionally, or spiritually, we treat it as a crisis to be managed case by case. The individual clergy experiencing these crises are made to feel like this is a personal failure on their part. Meanwhile, middle judicatory executives run themselves ragged responding to the numerous clergy crises within their jurisdiction. Many do not think they have the time, energy, or resources to provide their clergy with a comprehensive care program plus seminars or workshops aimed at preventing clergy breakdowns.

How different life would be in the church if church leaders would acknowledge right from the start that clergy, no matter how healthy and competent they are at the time of ordination, are going to break down from time to time. Some clergy would break down even if we sent them into the healthiest of parishes. But the reality is that some congregations have an unconscious commitment to remain destructive communities, chewing up all the clergy we can send them. I continue to be amazed at the courageous and possibly naive assumption on the part of these clergy that they can heal the neuroses of these congregations and once again make them attractive communities of faith. We don't even teach these pastors how to survive in some of these congregations; we certainly don't provide them with skills and strategies for helping them move beyond their destructive behavior.

The following are some of the things we should anticipate will happen to the clergy we ordain and send into ministry:

— Some will be unable to endure the stress of ministry and will experience physical and emotional breakdown.

— Approximately a quarter of these clergy will experience a failed marriage.

— Within the first ten years of parish ministry, roughly half will either be fired by their congregations or forced to move. Another fifteen percent will be forced out of their parishes during the last ten years of ministry. I have yet to see one denomination with a program of financial support for clergy who get fired.

— Some will lose their sense of call and begin placing money and status above the goals of the kingdom.

— Some will lose all sense of physical stewardship and allow their bodies to balloon to double their normal weight—making them far less credible healers in their members' eyes.

— Some will get so caught up in ministry successes and workaholic behavior that they will cease being good models of Grace.

— Some will enter new parishes and "shoot themselves in the foot" in the first six months through serious mistakes in judgment.

— Some will burn out and become exhausted, cynical, disillusioned, self-deprecating clergy.

— Some are simply not suited for parish ministry and will need a way to exit gracefully.

— Some will experience personal tragedy and be unable to function for a number of months.

— Some are going to be caught in sexual malfeasance.

— Some are simply going to die trying to be effective clergy.

Recognizing that these things are going to happen to clergy, why don't we put in place support systems and emergency care programs? Why aren't we doing more in prevention? No army would ever send soldiers into battle without a carefully thought out plan for dealing with war's casualties.

Imagine for a moment the unlikely possibility that clergy would graduate from seminary and begin bargaining with denominations who would court their employment. Among other things, they would look at the professional support programs available in each denomination. How well would your denomination fare? What programs of care for the caregiver could you offer? Having come through a twenty-year period during which we had a surplus of clergy applying for ministry in congregations, some seem to have concluded that we didn't need to concern ourselves here!

If you are concerned about these questions, you have come to the right resource. Gary Harbaugh has conducted a solid study of care giving practices within denominations. In addition to helping you get a fix on the type and style of caregiving your denomination offers, he also provides you with a road map for how to begin raising the quality of that caregiving.

What struck me immediately about Gary's work is his basic assertion that church growth and clergy caregiving are intimately related. Many of our congregations will not grow because we have a wounded caregiver trying to offer care to others with few or no resources to draw on for him- or herself.

Gary is an old friend, colleague, co-author, and fellow INFP. I am delighted he has turned his thoroughness, vision, and writing skill to this subject. We will all fare better in the future because of this work.

Roy M. Oswald

ACKNOWLEDGMENTS

The following have been particularly helpful in making possible my ministry of research and writing. I deeply appreciate the support of James Wind and the Lilly Endowment, Lavern Franzen, Susan Gamelin, Judy Eurton, Jean Burris, Craig Settlage, Joseph O'Neill, Daniel Aleshire, Thomas Blevins, Joseph Wagner, Kenneth Sauer, Gerald Troutman, Hermann Kuhlmann, Celia Hahn, Theresa Warner, Marlene Harbaugh, Loxi Dailey, Susan Stover, Dean James Childs and President Dennis Anderson of Trinity Lutheran Seminary. Thank you all.

INTRODUCTION

Ten years ago you would have had difficulty finding a workshop on *Caring for the Caregiver*. In fact, few professional schools in *any* caregiving vocation taught much about the critical importance of care for the caregiver.

Traditional seminaries tended to focus on preparation for the ministerial role. Seminarians typically were taught that vocational commitment required one to be selfless, not concerned about taking care of oneself, but rather to be devoted to the care of others. This devotion also meant that the pastor should not be assertive, even about such basics as salary, housing, or a day off.

Even today, some people believe that any emphasis on caring for the caregiver accents the wrong syllable.

In strong contrast to this ambivalence about caring for the caregiver is the virtually unanimous support for church growth. True, there are those who are uneasy about certain church growth *programs*, especially those that seem to smack of works righteousness. Nonetheless, while there may be disagreement about the *methods* used, the *idea* of church growth is affirmed by almost all.

What is not so commonly perceived is that caring for the caregiver and church growth are not only compatible, they are inextricably linked. Church growth wisely and faithfully goes hand-in-hand with a commitment to care for the caregiver! While this book focuses on what it means to care for the caregiver, the discerning reader will be aware of this underlying theme—the pivotal relationship between a growing person in ministry and a growing congregation.

Because church growth and the support of church leaders are integrally related, growth comes through caring, mission through ministry.

This is true whether the direction of the growth is in the breadth of the mission or the depth of the ministry. And the spirituality of the entire community of believers is strengthened and deepened when the ministry is one of caring mutuality.

Caring for the Caregiver is written for laypersons and lay leaders as well as for clergy and other full-time persons in ministry. Ministry is a partnership. When there is care for the caregiver and caring by the caregiver, God gives the growth. (I Cor. 3:6).

CHAPTER I

Another Perspective on Church Growth

Meet Jonathan and Joan.* They do not know each other. Each is a professional religious leader, but from different religious groups, and they serve in different parts of the country. Throughout the book we will see Jonathan and Joan in a variety of circumstances that religious leaders of all denominations and congregations face.

Although Joan and Jonathan learned a different theology in their seminaries, in two areas they had similar experiences. First, both studied the church growth movement. John's seminary teachers were generally supportive of the church growth movement; Joan's questioned some of the assumptions and methods of that movement, but affirmed the intention. Second, both Jonathan and Joan were taught that professional church leaders need personal as well as professional support.

Joan and Jonathan both heard about church growth issues in one class and about the importance of caring for the caregiver in another. No one suggested the close relationship of the two issues.

Is caring for the caregiver related to church growth? To answer that question, we must acknowledge that there is more than one way to look at church growth.

John's seminary stressed the biblical basis for church growth concerns, most often presented as Matthew 28:19-20:

"Go, therefore, and make disciples . . ."

---

* John and Joan are true-to-life, but not actual persons. The pastoral situations are purely hypothetical and should not be attributed to any specific congregation.

He was taught that church growth is fueled by "obedience to our Lord's command" and a sincere, contagious evangelistic zeal.

Joan was taught a humanistic approach that reflects an assumption about the inherent value of growth. This value at least partly underlies catchy sayings such as:

A happy church is a growing church.
A growing church is a happy church.

At her seminary Joan learned that growth is a very natural interest and human concern. Growth is genetically "programmed" into our physical bodies and we anticipate intellectual, emotional, social, and spiritual growth in children and (depending on which developmental theorist we read) in adults. Reaching for growth also reflects a human desire to share with others that which is meaningful to us. When others share our convictions, their value is affirmed.

Both Jonathan and Joan learned that concern for church growth is not new; the impetus to attract others to the faith is as old as faith itself. Sometimes the focus of church growth is on numbers (breadth), sometimes on spiritual development (depth). Of course, both breadth and depth are needed. Throughout Christian history there have been times both for spreading the seed and for gathering in the harvest, times when the emphasis has been mission and times when it has been ministry.

We know that church growth does not occur in a vacuum. Jonathan was taught that only the Spirit gives growth; we can spread the seed and water it, but God alone gives the growth (I Cor. 3:6). Joan learned about growth from a psychological perspective—that there must be a "readiness" factor before the seed can take root. She also learned to consider sociological factors. What is going on in society as a whole will also affect the response of people to the proclamation of the gospel at any given time in that culture's history.

These, then, are the two primary ways to look at church growth, biblical and theological or psychological and sociocultural. But there is one common and strong thread between these approaches. Both Jonathan and Joan were taught that the emphasis in church growth is placed on *outcome*.

Church Growth and the Professional Leader

But there is another way to look at church growth. That is to emphasize *process*. What is the *dynamic* of church growth? What moves a congregation toward growth? How does the church leader affect church growth? Are some leaders more effective than others?

The leadership question is a crucial one. Some say leadership has "everything" to do with church growth. In fact, there are those in the church growth movement who believe that a church does not really grow unless the leader wants it to! Many believe that a strong leader who empowers lay persons to evangelize others is the key to growth.

This emphasis on leadership makes sense. Most persons familiar with basic group dynamics would agree that the leader is the key to group functioning. The health and vitality of the group largely depends on the capacity of the leader. Providing leadership for outreach and assimilation of new members is an important aspect in the life of any church. The church leader is responsible for empowering the laity for the aspects of ministry that lead to church growth.

Less obvious is that the health and well-being of Jonathan and Joan are essential to their ongoing effectiveness as leaders. Perhaps this reality is obscured by the assumption that the leader is a leader. The pastor is a pastor. It is not always as apparent that the professional leader is a person with physical, psychological, and spiritual challenges like any other human being.

The Person in Ministry

Ten years ago there were few seminaries that offered even a single course on the pastor as a *person*. Conventional wisdom was that seminarians were people preparing for ministry. Therefore the thrust of theological training was not on the person, but on the person in *ministry*. It still is.

Most seminaries teach the classical disciplines: Bible, Systematic Theology, and Church History. The applied ministry studies, like pastoral care and counseling, provide some perspective on personal issues that might affect ministry. But even there the emphasis is on the care and counseling of others, rather than on the one who ministers. Furthermore, while pastoral care courses are popular electives, Jonathan was *required* to take only one and Joan only two while in seminary.

Even less likely to be seen in a theological school curriculum is a specific *course* on the *person* in ministry. In fairness to seminaries, there is a great deal that judicatories expect a graduate to know upon graduation. No one wants a leader who has been poorly prepared in Biblical studies, theology, or church history. In the rush to teach traditional curriculum, it is easy to see how seminaries would prefer to assume that seminarians can *independently* integrate personhood and ministry. That, however, is a very big and potentially faulty assumption!

But personal integration is very tough work when one is being exposed to the height and depth and length and breadth of a good theological education. When Joan's previous understandings are challenged and John's mind is stretched, there is bound to be, in the words of a popular song, "a whole lot of shakin' goin' on." How all of that "shakin" comes together for Joan and Jonathan as they prepare for ministry will affect both their personal self-understanding and leadership style—probably in quite different ways.

Is church growth related at all to the adequate preparation of *persons* in ministry? Only if church growth is related to the effectiveness of the professional leader.

And it most certainly is!

Where to Begin, What To Do

At best, seminaries can only start this process. Judicatories, colleagues in ministry, and congregations need to turn attention to the health and well-being of church leaders.

Before asking what we might do, we should ask "What is *already* being done by judicatories, colleagues, and congregations to care for the caregiver?" Can we learn anything by looking back in history and also by looking around us to see what is now taking place? How are present professional leadership support programs structured and how might we enhance future efforts?

CHAPTER II

Caring for the Caregiver

Caring for the caregiver is not a new concern. The group of disciples that gathered around Jesus and the apostles offered different kinds of personal support and care. The Pauline and Pastoral Epistles encourage early Christians to be supportive of those serving them.

Throughout Christian history there have been many examples of ways in which the caregiver received care. Monasticism can be understood in part as mutual caregiving in the context of Christian community. There were also very individual experiences and expressions of care. Luther had his Staupitz and then his Bugenhagen. Melanchthon had his Luther. Calvin had his Bucer. John Wesley had his brother, Charles, and George Whitefield.

What is meant by care, as seen in these examples, can differ greatly. Sometimes care means personal support. Jesus drew to himself all of the apostles and disciples, but there seemed to be a special supportive relationship with Peter, James, and John. The Apostle Paul appreciated those persons who provided personal support, but he also spoke of a general need for the material support of caregivers (I Cor. 9; I Tim. 5:18). St. Paul personally seemed especially supportive of Timothy. Staupitz was important in Luther's earlier life and Bugenhagen later became his confessor.

More *focused* attention on caring for caregivers has emerged relatively recently. Recognition of the *need* to care for the caregiver predated any organized efforts to do so. In 1955 Wayne Oates, one of the pioneers in the pastoral care movement, wrote *The Minister's Own Mental Health*. Oates' work meant a lot to me as I was preparing for parish ministry in the early 1960's. So did the works of Paul Tournier, Anton Boisen, Granger Westberg, Elisabeth Kubler-Ross, and Paul Tillich.

They and many others helped shape my reflections on persons and care-givers when I wrote *Pastor as Person* in 1984.

As of the mid-1980s, however, nearly thirty years after *The Minister's Own Mental Health* was published, there still was very little available literature on the person in ministry or on caring for the care-giver. The Alban Institute was one of the few places where seminarians like Joan or Jonathan or experienced professionals could look for sensitive treatment of the dynamics between the person of the caregiver and that person's ministry.

Beyond the Boundary

Not surprisingly, therefore, one of the earliest efforts to compare support programs across denominational lines was *Beyond the Boundary* in 1985. Coauthored by representatives of three different denominations and a senior Alban Institute consultant, *Beyond the Boundary* described ways that Presbyterians, Methodists, Episcopalians, and Lutherans provide support during the first few transitional years after individuals enter full-time ministry.

Beyond the Boundary was descriptive, not evaluative. Through accurate description of what different denominations were doing to ease the transition into the parish, judicatories could recognize and affirm their own approaches while noting the strengths of alternative models used by other denominations.

Beyond the Boundary indicated that more was taking place to address the transitional needs of new ministers than most people realized. The knowledge that other judicatories also recognized the special needs of those in the early years of ministry encouraged supportive denominational efforts.

Jonathan, Joan, and their peers greatly benefited from the "boundary" research. Judicatories acted upon the research conclusions that "formal programs targeted for newly ordained clergy are a real need," and that these programs are most helpful when they begin within a few months of entry into ordained ministry. The study also concluded that all new clergy should be invited to participate in transitional support programs. The research suggested that particular attention be given to newly ordained women.

Perhaps the most helpful outcome of the research was the concrete identification of how personal life and ministry are related. For example, the research found that the overall quality of a professional leader's personal life is affected by whether or not there had been an effective transition from the seminary to the parish. Single persons, spouses, and family members all have special needs, and good preventive work is essential to reduce the need for the time-consuming complexities of crisis intervention. Nurturing spirituality is also important during the transition into ministry and follow-up spiritual support is needed even after the transition is completed. Similarly, ongoing support by experienced clergy colleagues and lay committees in local congregations is crucial during and beyond the transitional years.

Beyond the Boundary noted that ongoing support from the seminary was important, but the ministry of the judicatory during the first few transitional years was even more significant. *Beyond the Boundary* ventured to conclude "whatever help is given to new pastors struggling with their boundary issues is experienced as a grace-full gift. Such a timely gift from the judicatory enables those same pastors, beyond the boundary, to give all the more of themselves to the church."

Life Beyond the Boundary

In their respective seminaries, both Joan and Jonathan knew about the work of The Alban Institute. They also heard about the Association of Theological Schools (ATS). John's seminary used the ATS "Readiness for Ministry" materials. Joan had taken the Theological School Inventory during her first seminary year.

Unknown either to Jonathan or Joan was the ongoing interest and support of ATS's work by the Lilly Endowment. In the summer of 1990, in the context of a discussion about the most effective ways to care for the caregiver, Dr. James Wind of the Endowment encouraged the initiation of a study of denominational programs supporting established professional church leaders (those beyond the transition stage). The kind of "support" in question was personal care and counseling for professional leaders and their families.

To begin the study of *Caring for the Caregiver*, a professional leadership support survey was developed to be used as a type of

structured interview with different denominations and religious bodies.
The survey (see Appendix I) explored the following questions:

What professional leadership counseling support is available?
How is it coordinated?
How are the costs covered?
What care and counseling resources are available?
How confidential is the support?
How comprehensive?
What kinds of resources are available if specialized care is needed?
What concerns do professional leaders or their families have about
    using the support offered?
What approach to support do judicatories prefer?
What types of "preventive" continuing education are offered?
What local support options are encouraged?
Given the limitations of financial resources, what forms of
    leadership support do judicatories consider absolutely essential?

As with the *Beyond the Boundary* study of transition support programs, the *Caring for the Caregiver* study was intended to be descriptive, not evaluative. The study set out to describe what church leaders like Jonathan or Joan would have available to them in the way of personal support, depending upon their denomination or judicatory.

In the chapters that follow, various forms of support and alternative approaches are described by denomination. The focus is on differences in polity and administration of support systems rather than on differences in theological doctrine.

Support is available to professional leaders at different levels. Does the polity of a religious body affect what kind of support is available and where would Joan or Jonathan most likely find it? What types of support cut across denominational lines?

Personal differences can also affect the provision of leadership support. Does it matter that Joan is a female and Jonathan is a male? Would it make a difference if they were single or married? In a solo or staff ministry? When times were generally good, or in a situation of transition or conflict?

Let's now turn to the first way to respond to the question of support. Does the religious body to which the professional leader belongs make a difference in what support is available?

CHAPTER III

Sixteen Ways of Caring

How many religious bodies have a nationally coordinated support program for professional leaders? Relatively few. If you are surprised, you're not alone. In the area of professional leadership support, it is natural for a Lutheran pastor to ask, "What do Methodists do to support their leaders?" or for a Methodist minister to ask the same question about Roman Catholics or Presbyterians.

The *Caring for the Caregiver* study found that there were relatively few religious groups with nationally coordinated support programs. For example, not all districts within Methodism approach leadership care in exactly the same way. Neither do all dioceses within the Roman Catholic Church nor all presbyteries within the Presbyterian Church.

In the descriptions that follow, nationally coordinated professional leadership care and counseling support programs are identified. When a religious body had no nationally coordinated care and counseling program, individual dioceses, presbyteries, synods or conferences that have representative programs are described.

There are several limitations to keep in mind when reading about the sixteen ways of caring for professional leaders. When the programs of a particular diocese or conference are described, please remember that they cannot fairly be generalized to the entire denomination or religious body. The specific example provides one angle of vision on that religious group's approach to leadership support, but another diocese or conference within that same denomination might address the issue in an entirely different manner.

Also, please remember that there are many more than sixteen religious bodies in the country. If every religious denomination or religious group had a nationally coordinated approach to care, the number of descriptions would fill a very big book. While the following sixteen ways of caring are intended to expand our vision of how to care for caregivers, the approaches described certainly do not exhaust the possibilities.

Recognize also that some of the sixteen ways are described in far greater detail than others. This does not represent any judgment about the inherent value of one approach over another. Rather, disparities in detail relate to the amount of information provided in the interviews.

Assumptions are important in any study. This study makes no assumption that there is one "best" way to provide leadership support. However, it *is* assumed that we all can learn from other denominations and religious groups. Each approach that follows shares a common concern to be supportive and each angle of vision offers something special that is worth considering.

Angles of Vision: Ways of Caring for the Caregiver

Does the religious body to which the professional leader belongs make a difference in what support is available? Let's look at what Jonathan or Joan would experience, depending on which of the following religious bodies they served.

1. African Methodist Episcopal (AME)

If Jonathan were an AME pastor, he would be in a Bishop-led denomination. A General Conference is held every four years. During the interim, a Bishops' Council and a General Board oversee the church's nineteen Episcopal districts, worldwide.

Because the AME does not have a national office specifically charged with providing a support system for ministers, in times of need Jonathan would turn to whatever programs the presiding Bishop of his Episcopal district made available. If Jonathan were in the Third District (West Virginia, Western Pennsylvania, and Ohio), support could come through retreats, pastoral institutes, and similar growth experiences.

Support might also come directly from the Bishop, who is known as the chief pastor. If he were not comfortable getting guidance form his

Bishop, Jonathan might seek out a fellow pastor or look for a counselor in the community. While there is medical insurance through the AME church, there is no insurance to cover counseling costs, so Jonathan would have to find a way to handle those himself.

2. The American Baptist Churches in the USA

Were Jonathan an American Baptist pastor, he would know about the three centers for career development and ministry. These ecumenical centers located in the East, Midwest, and the Far West are sponsored by the Missionaries Benefit Board of The American Baptist Churches in the USA for the use of their professional leaders.

In addition to the career and counseling centers, the American Baptist Church also has a Minister's Council, a professional society whose purpose is the advocacy and support of clergy and their families. Jonathan could order materials from the denomination's Valley Forge office, and he probably would know about a recent publication on clergy family issues, *The Stained Glass Fishbowl*, edited by Harley Hunt.

The American Baptist Church is divided into thirty-five regions, each having an Executive Minister who serves as a staff person on a Commission for Ministry. The Commission is primarily a think tank that deals with issues concerning clergy and families, issues of sexuality, singles in ministry, clergy couples in ministry, etc. While the American Baptist approach to professional leadership support is available region-ally, local implementation is up to the individual congregation. Most regions also identify local pastoral counselors.

If Jonathan ran into trouble, he would have a variety of options available to him. If his problems came to the attention of his judicatory, the typical response probably would be referral to the closest regional center. Financial assistance would be available through the denomina-tional Missionaries Benefit Board.

3. Progressive National Baptist Convention

The situation would be different if Jonathan were a member of The Progressive National Baptist Convention. This predominantly African-

American religious body holds an annual meeting to discuss directions in ministry. The Convention, however, does not govern its members; local congregations are completely autonomous. Therefore, care for the caregiver is not nationally coordinated.

As on example of local support, African-American professional leaders within the Progressive National Baptist Convention in Columbus, Ohio, could attend the Columbus Baptist Pastors' Conference. This includes all national affiliations of African-American Baptist groups (The Progressive National Baptist Convention, the National Baptist Convention, Inc., and the National Baptist Convention, unincorporated). This Conference of about fifty male Black Baptist pastors meets once a month on Mondays, primarily for fellowship. On any Monday, about seventy percent of those eligible to attend are present.

A committee within the Conference deals with leadership support issues as needs arise. For example, sometimes there is debate on an issue of interest to all pastors, such as the role of authority. Or individual members may raise personal concerns and get ideas about possible referral resources in the community.

In addition to support from Conference members, the professional leader may consult a private counselor in the community. Private counseling may be the preferred route for those who find it hard to publicly acknowledge that "the helper needs help."

The amount of insurance coverage or other financial support available for private counseling depends on the professional leader's contract with the local congregation. Therefore, coverage may vary considerably from pastor to pastor and congregation to congregation.

The seminaries in the Columbus area also offer opportunities for continuing and preventive education.

4. Southern Baptist Convention

Were Jonathan one of the approximately 40,000 pastors of the Southern Baptist Convention, he would be of the free church tradition, which highly values congregational autonomy. Though there is freedom to approach leadership support in a variety of ways, the Southern Baptist Convention also highly values cooperation. Congregations voluntarily make financial contributions to a Cooperative Program, making some resources generally available for the support of pastors like Jonathan and his family.

One example is what is provided through the Mission Boards. The Home Mission Board in Atlanta has about 4,000 persons under its care; not all of them are pastors, some serve in social ministry or some other capacity. In addition to significant assessment services, the Home Mission Board provides ongoing support services. For example, the Board might fly Jonathan to Atlanta if he needed leadership support services or counseling. There also is a Foreign Missions Board in Richmond, Virginia, supporting missionary work in over 100 countries. Assessment and counseling is available for foreign as well as home missionaries.

Whether Jonathan is a pastor in Texas or Ohio, there is a local fellowship of churches within his geographical area. The local association relates to a state convention. At the state as well as the local level, resource persons are available to provide support and encouragement to pastors. For example, the Texas State Association has a designated person who oversees support services and a counseling service is provided for pastors. The Metro Columbus Baptist Association relates to the State Convention of Baptists in Ohio. In Ohio, there is an special fund to assist pastors with the costs of professional counseling beyond what insurance will cover. In Texas, Jonathan could request financial help for counseling expenses from the Annuity Board, where his request would be handled discreetly. He could also ask for the names of counselors.

Beyond the state convention, Jonathan could also look to the national retreat centers in North Carolina and New Mexico. They and the Sunday School Board in Nashville provide ongoing programs, some of which focus on pastors. The six seminaries also regularly offer continuing education programs for pastors.

5. The Christian Church (Disciples of Christ)

While The Christian Church (Disciples of Christ) has no national pastoral care program, if Joan were a Disciples minister, she would be able to find support services at the regional level. The same confidential, no-cost services are available for her family members as well.

At present, preventive programs are not offered, but if financial resources were available, those programs would be a priority. However, Joan would be encouraged to participate in a peer support group.

The Disciples see their independence as a strength. Every church is autonomous. There is, however, regional cooperation. For example, if Joan were in the Southwest Region (Texas, New Mexico, and Louisiana), she and her husband could receive counseling from a designated counselor. While the counselor receives a stipend from the denomination and provides a quarterly report of the number of ministers seen, Joan would not be named and no details would be given to the judicatory. Typically these counselors assist church leaders with a broad range of issues—grief reactions, problems with marriage or family, work overload and burnout, frustration with ministry as a profession, frustration with lay leadership, and frustration with judicatory leaders. While the denomination covers the expenses of counseling without question, Joan can make a financial contribution to the counseling program.

6. The Church of God

The 1992 National Association of Evangelicals (NAE) Ministry to the Pastoral Family Award was given to the Pastoral Crisis Intervention Program of the Church of God, Cleveland, Tennessee. In 1982, the NAE established a Task Force on the Family. Based on its belief that "the place to start in the recovery of the Christian family is with Christian leaders and their families," the Task Force proposed a resolution that was passed in 1988 by the NAE calling upon member denominations to:

> provide adequate resources to enable leaders and their spouses to meet the physical, economic, emotional, and spiritual needs of their families; to protect their leadership from unreasonable demands on their time, energy, and privacy; to be alert to what would thwart an effective ministry to church families and, in turn, weaken their ministries to the families of others.

The Church of God was recognized by the NAE for the work of its Office of Ministerial Care (OMC) in providing a confidential, toll-free telephone counseling hot-line, available from 8:00-12:00 a.m. and 1:00-5:00 p.m. (Eastern time), Monday through Friday. In 1991, the hot-line received 1,402 calls from pastors and families in need.

Through the Professional Referral System, assistance is provided in obtaining professional counseling near the geographical area in which the minister resides. Over 550 referrals were completed in 1991.

The OMC also provides pastoral support to ministers whose ministerial licenses have been terminated and designs or approves counseling programs for those who desire restoration to the ministry.

Often the Office of Ministerial Care is alerted that a ministerial family is in need of help. The OMC would then telephone Jonathan and ask how they could be of assistance. More than 1,600 telephone calls were made in connection with this service in 1991.

In addition to the intervention program and other support ministries, the OMC offers enrichment programs to help pastors and spouses cope with the stresses of ministry. There also is a retired ministers program that includes widowers and the widows of clergy. The OMC assists at the international level with missionary orientation, marriage and family enrichment, programs to help with specific cultural needs, and missionary debriefing.

Both stateside and overseas programs emphasize ways to avoid future crises. Enrichment (preventive) programs include "couples and family retreats, ministerial children's conferences, ministerial spouse's programs and other programs and resources which aid in strengthening the ministerial family."

A "State and Regional Manual" has been written to guide superintendents and regional overseers in the United States and overseas in their coordination of ministerial care programs. The superintendent or regional overseer has general responsibility for the well-being of ministers and their families in a specific geographical area, however in critical situations the OMC center in Cleveland may be the primary resource. The regional overseer may also identify experienced and specially trained pastors to assist with crisis counseling. Professional consultants are also engaged for providing counseling in more complex situations. These professionals (e.g., AAPC, AAMFT, ACPE, CAPS, etc.) are recommended by the state or regional overseer and must be approved by the OMC.

The Church of God has developed a plan for a new Ministerial Enrichment facility to be built during the 1990's. The facility will house a fully coordinated support ministry of clinical, enrichment, and ongoing care programs. Plans for a retreat center are also being developed.

7. The Eastern Orthodox Church

More than four million persons belong to the Eastern Orthodox Church in the United States. While all Eastern Orthodox churches embrace orthodoxy (correct, true or straight belief, path or worship), there may be significant jurisdictional or ethnic differences between the various bodies. Some of these differences can be inferred simply from their names: Antiochian, Carpathorussian, Russian, Greek, Macedonian, Serbian, Ethiopian, and Ukranian Orthodox Churches. Furthermore, there is a distinction between those Orthodox churches canonically united with Constantinople and those which are separated from that communion.

Let's look at what Jonathan might experience if he were a priest in the Eastern Orthodox Christian Church in America, as compared to the Greek Orthodox Church. The Eastern Orthodox Christian Church is of the old Eastern rite and has a Ukranian background. As a priest, Father Jonathan might be married and hold a secular job alongside of his priestly vocation. He probably would serve a small parish and receive a stipend. In a larger parish a parsonage might be provided.

Jonathan may or may not have pension and health benefits through an insurance affiliation of the national church. Participation is voluntary and Jonathan might choose to rely on the benefits package of his secular work.

Were Jonathan, his wife, or family to have a problem, they would pray for guidance and perhaps consult their Archbishop or the Metropolitan in New Jersey. They also would be free to consult a community counselor for confidential counseling, with no report going to the Archbishop or Metropolitan.

Another source of potential support for Jonathan in difficult times would be his parish council. However, Jonathan would find few options for support from colleagues, simply because of the limited number of Eastern Orthodox congregations in most areas. He would need to rely on whatever continuing education is offered in the community since his branch of the Eastern Orthodox Church has no formally organized preventive education programs.

The situation would be different if Jonathan were a Greek Orthodox priest. While there are Eastern Orthodox seminaries in New York, Pennsylvania, Alaska, and Greece, Jonathan would probably be a graduate of Holy Cross Greek Orthodox Theological School in Massachusetts, which prepares men to become priests for the Archdiocese of North and South America. In addition to being a center of learning, Holy Cross Seminary is the home of Holy Cross Press, which disseminates literature and information about Greek Orthodoxy. The seminary also has a counseling staff and has been developing psychological profiles of seminary students in order to facilitate their adjustment to parish ministry.

There have been many changes within the Greek Orthodox Church in the past fifty years. A generation ago there was virtually no English spoken in the Divine Liturgy and many of the priests were from Greece. In the last twenty years or so theological training has become essential and at Holy Cross that training now includes studies in pastoral care and field education. Even with this climate of change in the church, Jonathan would have to be prepared for considerable parochialism in ethnic parishes. Many of the members of these parishes struggle with the challenges of integrating modern life and traditional family structure and culture. Seminary education now is attempting to prepare priests for the diversity their ministries might involve.

Most Greek Orthodox priests are married. A priest who aspires to be a Bishop or Archbishop remains unmarried, as do a small percentage who choose to remain celibate for other reasons. Those in parish ministry and their families are eligible for an Archdiocese health program, which provides pension and health benefits. While encouraged to use this national health plan for clergy, parishes have the freedom to choose to provide these benefits through local resources.

There is no diocesan counselor, as such, but there are counselors in some communities who are sensitive to the religious and ethnic backgrounds of Orthodox laypersons and priests. If Jonathan sought a counselor on his own, the counseling would be confidential. If his Bishop thought he needed counseling and asked him to take a leave of absence, the Bishop might require a counseling report before Jonathan would be permitted to return to his parish ministry.

Each of the eight Greek Orthodox dioceses in the United States may be administered somewhat differently by their Bishops. If Jonathan served in West Virginia (the Diocese of Pittsburgh), he would meet with his fellow orthodox clergy four times a year for an overnight retreat. They would discuss theological and pastoral issues, and there might be some continuing education. Peer support is considered important in this diocese.

Jonathan might also take a three-month sabbatical for which he would be eligible after five years in the parish. The sabbatical is optional, and the parish must be able to financially support it. With the sabbatical program, and expanding vacation periods after each five years of parish ministry, Father Jonathan would see his Church trying to be supportive of him and his family in concrete ways.

8. The Episcopal Church

Within the Episcopal Church, each of the 110 diocesan offices handles the problems of Episcopal priests and their families. While there is communication and assistance available from the national denominational office, each diocese is autonomous. Professional leadership support typically is through a denominational version of an employee assistance program.

The Diocese of Chicago provides an example of a diocesan program. While other dioceses may have similar programs, the Bishop is key to what is offered in any particular diocese.

In terms of clergy, Chicago is one of the largest of dioceses and it has a proactive program of professional leadership support. There are over 600 professional leaders and, with family members, 1,200 or more who are eligible for support services. If Joan were a priest in crisis, she would have two choices. She could independently select her own counselor, or she could contact the designated resource person and go through the referral process.

Joan might choose the second alternative since it offers a distinct financial advantage. The diocese utilizes a managed care program, which means that seventy percent of Joan's costs will be reimbursed if she uses a counselor within the program. If Joan selects a a counselor outside the managed care system, she will be required to pay fifty percent of her costs. The maximum yearly benefit is also about one-third lower if an independent counselor is used.

Let's say Joan (or a member of her family) contacted the designated diocesan resource person and was referred to the managed care program. She could talk with a counselor by telephone or in person and receive a referral to the provider network.

Joan would have access to an extensive provider network. Pastoral counselors (AAPC), licensed clinical social workers, Ph.D. clinical psychologists, psychiatrists, and Masters level psychiatric nurses and Masters level clinical members of the American Association of Marriage and Family Therapists (AAMFT) are all available through the managed care system.

When inpatient care is needed, decisions are made on a case-by-case basis. For example, in situations involving chemical dependency, the diocese prefers for the professional leader to enter a 28-day inpatient program. The reason for this is that even if Joan tells her congregation about her enrollment in an outpatient program, her parishioners may not give her the time and space she requires to work on her treatment plan.

In addition to providing appropriate support to the professional leader, during a 28-day program there is also opportunity for the diocese to work with the congregation on group recovery, since the congregation may have dynamics similar to that of a co-dependent family.

When a priest has a problem with alcohol, some members of the congregation may contact the diocesan resource person. An intervention is planned, and if successful, the priest goes into treatment (there are a number of appropriate treatment facilities with which the diocese has a prior working relationship). Then the diocesan resource person returns to the congregation, explains the leave of absence and discusses personnel implications. The priest's salary and benefits continue without interruption. Parish needs are identified and an interim priest is appointed to assume pastoral responsibilities.

Then the diocesan resource person meets with the congregation in an open forum meeting and tells the congregation why the priest is away. Just five or six years ago the reasons for the priest's absence were not directly discussed, but experience has proven that credibility is lost by not being open and honest. The priest knows that the congregation will be told about the alcohol treatment (although the specifics about family stresses, etc., are not shared with the congregation). The diocesan resource person holds one or two forums on chemical dependency and treatment, utilizing films, videos, and other materials.

To be able to provide such services, the diocesan resource person must have certain competencies. The present resource person in the Chicago Diocese is a priest with a background in family counseling. She has also taught family issues in nursing at a junior college and has training and experience in alcoholism counseling.

Joan might also find herself in the midst of a serious congregational conflict. In the Chicago diocese, there is an office of Congregational Development with whom the diocesan resource person works very closely. A team is assembled to work with the congregation in crisis and the diocesan resource person may be one of the members of that team.

If Joan's congregation was in crisis, she would automatically be referred to the diocesan resource person's office. The purpose is not to determine whether Joan or someone else is to blame, but to assure her that an external network of support is available. Referral for short term, confidential mental health services might be offered to help her manage the stress. If Joan accepted the referral, no information would come from the mental health professional to the diocesan resource person.

In the Chicago diocese, the staff reports directly to the Bishop. Information is shared with the Bishop only with the priest's permission. The diocesan resource person is in a pivotal liaison position in matters of professional leadership support.

9. Reform Judaism

While not coordinated from a national office, Reform Judaism makes support programs for the personal care and counseling of professional leaders available at both the national and regional levels. If Jonathan were a rabbi, the same counseling and therapy services available to him would be available to his wife and other family members. Insurance covers confidential private therapy, although coverage varies from location to location; participation in the insurance plan of the Central Conference is voluntary. One alternative some rabbis take is to become members of a health maintenance organization (HMO).

Just as in most of the Christian denominations, there is no one specific program that has national endorsement for such concerns as substance abuse, sexual misconduct, financial impropriety, career development, or outplacement to secular work. Nor is there a national psycho-diagnostic center or inpatient/residential care facility.

Psychotherapy is a recognized resource for religious leaders. Many rabbis prefer private therapy where there are no concerns for confidentiality nor potential impact on present job security or future vocational mobility.

Jonathan and his spouse would have the opportunity to attend a program related to congregational life (conflict management, leadership, etc.) or spirituality about once or twice a year. Rabbis can take advantage of a midcareer review program, designed to help them gain perspective on their rabbinic calling.

Locally, peer support groups are encouraged but, as in other religious bodies, not every professional leader attends. Leader-layperson committees within the synagogue may or may not be perceived as a helpful resource.

Since 1978, the national rabbinic organization (the Central Conference of American Rabbis or CCAR) has sponsored a "hotline" coordinated by a rabbi with psychological training. The hotline is a crisis intervention resource for rabbis, their spouses, and children. Sometimes referrals will be made to a network of rabbis who are geographically distributed throughout the country, assuming someone in the network is within reasonable traveling distance. These network rabbis are trained in counseling. A person can be referred to one of these counselors for up to three face-to-face counseling sessions without cost. After three sessions the network rabbi would either make a referral to a counselor outside the network or continue to see the person on a fee-for-service basis.

It is noteworthy that the Conservative rabbinate has started a similar program.

Additional resources available for professional leaders and their families include the Jewish Family and Children's Service. This agency offers services across the branches of Judaism, providing mental health support, counseling, and therapy throughout the country. Services are provided on a private fee-for-service basis.

10. Evangelical Lutheran Church in America

If Joan and Jonathan were pastors or Associates in Ministry in the Evangelical Lutheran Church in America (ELCA), they would probably be members of the self-insured health benefits program administered by the ELCA Board of Pensions. Ordained and lay professional leaders who have alternative insurance coverage are not required to be covered under the Board of Pensions.

After a deductible is met, mental health coverage for Board of Pensions members pays approximately 60 percent of the cost of treatment. To be covered, services must be provided by a licensed psychiatrist, a licensed doctoral level psychologist, or a qualified counselor under the direct supervision of a psychiatrist or psychologist. Jonathan or Joan would be free to choose any qualified counselor and the counseling would be completely confidential. However, to be covered under the health benefits plan, the condition must have a psychiatric diagnosis. Marital counseling, therefore, is not a covered service.

While the Board of Pensions medical benefits program is church-wide, the various synods of the church may supplement benefits. For example, some synods offer counseling resources or financial assistance for marriage counseling. Or, in situations of financial hardship, some synods assist with the deductible and copayments for a Board of Pensions covered expense.

ELCA Regional Pastoral Care Programs

The merger that created the ELCA has produced an additional professional leadership support program. The ELCA divided the synods into nine regions. Some of these regions implemented a pastoral care support program as an extension of the Bishop's office that offers a multidisciplinary psychodiagnostic assessment to professional leaders (clergy and full-time lay Associates in Ministry) and their family members.

KAIROS CARE AND COUNSELING℠ is an example of an ELCA Regional Pastoral Care Program. Kairos is the designated resource to provide support services to professional leaders of Region Six (Ohio, Michigan, Indiana, Kentucky), and Region Nine (Virginia, North Carolina, South Carolina, Tennessee, Alabama, Georgia, Mississippi, Florida-Bahamas, and the Caribbean). Any of the twelve synods in these regions can refer professional leaders to Columbus, Ohio or Orlando, Florida for a two-day assessment of physical, intellectual, emotional, interpersonal, and vocational concerns within the context of faith. Psychiatric, psychological, psychosocial, and pastoral perspectives are brought to bear on whatever issues are identified, with a goal of greater personal and spiritual integration.

However, the Regional Pastoral Care Program does not replace the individual services covered by the Board of Pensions, nor does it replace any existing resources of individual synods. Rather, it serves as an additional resource for initial diagnostic evaluation and assessment prior to referral to more local resources or as a second opinion.

In most instances of referral by a synod, however, the professional leader sees the program as one of partnership with the synod and an extension of the Bishop's pastoral concern. There is an expectation that something will come out of the assessment that will be helpful for both the individual and the bishop as they consider together how best to address whatever problems exist. If, after the evaluation is completed, that partnership is reaffirmed through informed consent, then the summary written for the professional leader is shared with the referring bishop. The synod is usually in a good position to help the professional leader implement the recommendations of the Pastoral Care team, but the choice of whether or not to share the consultation summary is up to the professional leader.

In the regional program the entire cost of the assessment is covered. The Board of Pensions and the referring synod combine resources to cover any deductible or co-payment. The only expense for the professional leader is that of travel and lodging. Sometimes the referring synod covers those expenses as well.

Joan and Jonathan might also have the opportunity to participate in one of the preventive educational workshops available through Kairos Care and Counseling. Some of the synods of Region Six and Region Nine have sponsored one-day workshops on the Pastor as Person, the Person in Ministry (includes lay ministers and spouses of professional leaders), Personality and Faith (personal growth in spirituality), the Myers-Briggs and Ministry, and God's Gifted People (leadership applications to church councils, mutual ministry committees, etc.). Other preventive programs have covered communication skills and relationship building for professional leaders and spouses, effective teamwork in multiple staff ministries, and transitions and losses. These preventive programs are intended to address concerns and problems before they reach the crisis level.

11. The Lutheran Church–Missouri Synod

The LC-MS has undergone a transition in its approach to the provision of care and counseling for professional leaders and their families. Until recently, only some LC-MS districts offered coordinated support programs and regional differences were significant.

The situation today is far different. There is now an Office of Ministerial Health/Health and Healing in St. Louis. On January 1, 1992, the LC-MS Worker Benefit Plans initiated a managed mental health care program to maximize benefits for mental health and substance abuse care. Coverage under the Concordia Health Plan for outpatient expenses is now 100 percent for the first ten visits, eighty percent for eleven-twenty visits, and fifty percent for twenty-one to fifty visits. Inpatient, residential treatment and day treatment are covered at ninety percent.

Under the plan, services provided to professional leaders and their families are confidential. The managed health care program would cover expenses if Jonathan needed marriage or family counseling, although vocational counseling is not a covered expense.

Counselors eligible under the benefit provisions include licensed psychiatrists and doctoral level psychologists, licensed Masters level psychologists, MSW psychiatric social workers, AAPC Fellow and Diplomate Pastoral Counselors, and clinical members of the American Association of Marriage and Family Therapists (AAMFT).

Access to the program is through an 800 number. Jonathan would call the care management company and receive a referral to an appropriate counselor. Neither the managed care company nor the counselor makes a report to the district. An additional feature of the LC-MS program is that judicatory leaders may also call the managed care company and receive consultation on difficult pastoral care situations without compromising confidentiality.

Preventive continuing education programs vary from district to district, but may include topics such as marriage and family, spiritual growth, personal stress management and self-care, sexual ethics, and team or staff ministries. Some type of continuing education program that serves a preventive purpose is usually available every year or two in most districts.

Pan-Lutheran Programs

The following two approaches to leadership support have a relationship with and receive funds from both ELCA synods and Lutheran Church—Missouri Synod districts.

The CONSULTATION TO CLERGY program serves both the

ELCA and LC-MS in the Northwest, providing direct support ministry to professional leaders and their families and supplementing any other services covered by medical insurance. The program is a pastoral care outreach of the offices of the ELCA Bishops and LC-MS Presidents and offers referral to a network of primarily AAPC Pastoral Counselors.

As a pastoral care program, Consultation to Clergy is available anonymously and confidentially. No report is made to the judicatory unless prior arrangements have been made and agreed upon.

Consultation to Clergy works with other resources to provide vocational counseling. Some of that is done in a retreat setting, reflecting on vocational options. Outplacement counseling is also available.

Continuing education and preventive programs are offered several times a year in the areas of personal self-care, stress management, marriage, family, sexual ethics, chemical health, conflict management, team ministry, vocational transition, and spiritual growth. In addition, Consultation to Clergy encourages peer support groups and is coordinating a mentor program. At the local level, congregations are encouraged to have mutual ministry committees. Consultation to Clergy also provides some services to congregations, for example, when they are facing transition to a new pastor.

A second cooperative program between the ELCA and the Lutheran Church-Missouri Synod is CLERGY CARE, an arm of Lutheran Social Services in Texas. Counseling is available to clergy, spouses, families and other church workers at centers in Austin, Dallas-Ft. Worth, and Houston.

Clergy Care's *New Creation* newsletter, published about four times a year, contains articles relevant to the support of professional leaders (see Appendix III). For example, recent issues have dealt with family systems issues, the congregation as an emotional system, and leadership.

The ELCA, and LC-MS provide insurance coverage for services. In addition, there is Synod-District financial support for the program. Funds are available to assist individuals who cannot afford to meet deductibles or co-payments, or when insurance coverage is not applicable. No one is refused service because of inability to pay.

The director of the program is an AAPC pastoral counselor. Services of a psychiatrist are utilized for professional back-up and medication evaluations.

Services are completely confidential, if that is the desire of the counselee. While Bishops can make referrals to the program, the percentage of self-referrals is increasing. If a report is needed and the counselee is willing, the director arranges a meeting between the counselee, the Bishop and the counselor, and the counselee assumes the responsibility of sharing directly with the Bishop. This innovative approach has become the standard for reporting purposes.

Clergy Care is the primary resource for all counseling needs. When specialized care for needs such as substance abuse or sexual misconduct are required, referrals are made to other programs.

Clergy Care has a significant continuing education service, offering workshops in areas such as stress management, family concerns, and vocational and spiritual development. The director also has a consultation ministry to congregations. Utilizing insights from family systems theory, the director works with congregations experiencing dysfunction.

KAIROS CARE AND COUNSELING, CONSULTATION TO CLERG, and CLERGY CARE are three types of regionalized support programs. In any one of them, Jonathan and Joan would find a broad range of counseling and consultative services. Because there is both a regional and a more local emphasis, there is breadth but also flexibility to tailor offerings and responses to the needs of the specific areas and individuals served.

12. Mennonite

The Mennonites are of the free church tradition with considerable pastoral and congregational independence. Not all Mennonite ministers are affiliated with the General Conference, but if Jonathan were, he would have the benefit of coordinated national and local leadership support. Eighty percent of the cost of the program is funded by Mennonite Mutual Aid and 20 percent is paid by the professional leader.

Counselors from different disciplines are eligible to provide services, but must be supervised by a psychiatrist. There are also a number of Mennonite mental health centers and career development centers located around the country where Jonathan or members of his family could receive confidential counseling. Typical areas of concern professional leaders bring to counseling are how to survive in ministry, how to deal with depression, and how to resolve marital problems.

Preventive education is provided in the areas of marriage, sexual ethics, conflict management, staff ministries, and spirituality. Jonathan and his wife could attend such programs several times a year. Peer support groups are also encouraged, as are congregation-based support committees.

13. The United Methodist Church

At the national level, the United Methodist Church has a General Board of Higher Education and Ministry, responsible for higher education and colleges and ordained and diaconal ministries. There is also a division for diaconal ministry, consecrated layworkers who work full time, primarily in Christian education and youth work.

The Conference Board of Ordained Ministry in each annual conference (an annual Conference is a geographical area typically with approximately 500-700 ministers) sees seminarians through the ordination process. While it is a credentialing body, it also provides support systems for clergy and their families.

In each annual conference a group of about sixty-five churches is called a district. The district and the Conference Board are linked, and the national General Board communicates with them both.

While most of the professional leadership support takes place within the conferences and districts of the conferences, the national General Board sometimes helps to identify available resources. Since there is communication between the various Boards, the national office is able to have a general idea of what is happening in the conferences.

There are five jurisdictions in the country. Every four years the conferences send representatives to a jurisdictional training event for workshops and training of new officers coming onto the Conference Board.

Between jurisdictional events Conference Board chairpersons are surveyed. In the survey, there is a whole section on support systems, with questions such as:

Do you offer pre-retirement seminars?
Do you have a pastoral counselor for clergy and their families?
What are other resources you provide for clergy and their families?

What resources are available to respond to persons where gender or
cultural differences require special resources?

A recent survey indicated that four years ago a larger percentage of
clergy and their families were utilizing counseling through conference
offices than are today. To address that situation, more annual conferences now have insurance programs to cover the costs of outside counselors. This seems to be a more workable approach, since one single counselor cannot possibly meet the needs of all of those seeking assistance.

If Joan needed counseling, insurance would cover most of the cost.
Each annual conference is autonomous in insurance decisions; one conference may insure through the denomination's Board of Pensions,
another may select a commercial insurance company. Thus, there are
disparities in coverage between the conferences.

While there may be differences across conferences in coverage,
there are similarities in areas of concern. Sexual ethics is one common
concern, as is the divorce rate. Areas of special concern may be more
prevalent in one conference than another, such as the impact of the farm
crisis on those ministers serving in the Midwest.

The General Board provides resource and programming support to
the annual conferences. Present or recent programs include three retreat
models dealing with marriage in ministry. If Joan had been married
while in seminary, she would have had the opportunity to attend the first
retreat during her candidacy (after she declared she wanted to prepare for
ordained ministry). She and her spouse would have attended a second
retreat during the seminary years, and the final retreat after the first year
of ministry. The retreats utilize a family systems model, focusing on
spiritual formation and marriage enrichment.

Clergy couples represent a special population, and they are supported in a variety of ways after entering the field. There are approximately 1,000 clergy couples on the roster. The UMC has a clergy
couples association that publishes its own newsletter.

Every four years the United Methodist Church holds a consultation
for women clergy. Also, each year women faculty and administrators of
the thirteen UMC seminaries gather to share resources. In 1991, 10.5
percent of clergy in the UMC were female, with women making up 40.6
percent of Methodist seminarians. In recognition of this growing population, the UMC publishes a clergywoman's journal.

Attention is also given to the special concerns of ethnic women (Asian-American, African-American, Hispanic, Native American). For example, there is an Association of African United Methodist Episcopal women clergy. Recruitment of ethnic minorities is also a goal of the National Board.

Minorities of other kinds are also supported. Among those are clergy eligible for the Association of Physically Challenged Ministers. This is a relatively new support group that identifies resources and provides both education and opportunities for networking.

Other areas of programming offered in relation to annual conference Boards of Ministry include pre-retirement seminars. There is also a journal published four times a year for all retirees and their spouses.

Spiritual formation is an area of support for all professional leaders. At times, support is provided around particular areas of concern, such as sexual ethics or chemical dependency. The General Board and the annual conferences offer guidelines on sexual ethics, including how to deal with grievances and how to respond to victims and make restitution. Special training is offered in the area of sexual ethics, and is co-led by a male/female team. The participants return to their respective conferences to implement the model of support, consultation and victim advocacy.

Individual annual conferences also provide support for those affected by alcoholism and other chemical dependencies. The conferences utilize a variety of treatment approaches and facilities, depending on the type of pastoral support programs available within their geographic area. There is no single national treatment program or facility.

While there are many common concerns, and the resources of the General Board of Higher Education and Ministry are available to all, the individual conferences often take quite different directions in supporting professional leaders. The following two United Methodist approaches illustrate this diversity.

The Florida Conference of the UMC

The Florida Conference has a Board of Ordained Ministry, which must meet the national church's disciplinary requirements, but beyond that, develops its own guidelines for the support of professional leaders and their families. The counseling support of clergy, spouses, and families is under the direction of a Counseling Network Committee with a pastoral counselor as the committee consultant. Upon the recommendation of the consultant, counselors are approved by the Counseling Network Committee to provide confidential counseling services to church workers.

Each network counselor completes a detailed annual report on services to UMC clergy and their families. The report identifies client type, general categories of presenting problems, numbers of clients working with particular issues, the total number of persons counseled, the total number of counseling hours, the average fee per counseling hour, the total number of clients referred by referral sources, the number of new clients and the number of continuing clients, a tally of payment methods, whether or not the counselor desires to continue with the counseling network, and whether or not the counselor had professional, ethical, or legal difficulties during the year.

The resources provided through the Counseling Network in the Florida Conference are available to clergy, spouses, and their families and to other church workers.

If Jonathan were a pastor in the Florida Conference, he and his spouse would receive a newsletter three times a year covering issues relating to the counseling concerns of clergy. The newsletter helps to remind church workers that help is always available to them and their families. For approximately two years after a divorce, former spouses are included in the support programs available to professional leaders and their families.

The Florida Conference provides major medical coverage through the Board of Pensions of the UMC, which has a working relationship with a commercial insurance company. There is a preferred provider clause in the coverage, and the counselors in the counseling network are considered preferred providers. The preferred providers' services are covered at eighty percent for both church workers and family members. If Jonathan or a member of his family were to choose a counselor other than one on the preferred provider list, the Conference would pay seventy percent of the cost and Jonathan would pay thirty percent.

The insurance coverage is quite comprehensive, paying not only for diagnosable psychiatric disorders, but also for marriage, family, or career counseling provided by a licensed or approved network counselor.

The Counseling Network Committee offers a financial subsidy if either a counselee or a counselor member of the counseling network applies for funds. Subsidy funds totaled $7,000 in 1991. Financial help can also come from a national denominational offering called the Golden Cross, which may be used to offset medical and mental health expenses of clergy. The Conference had approximately $3,000 of Golden Cross funds available for special needs in 1991.

Other than through the counseling network, there are no specially identified facilities or resources for treatment of special needs, such as substance abuse, sexual misconduct, or financial impropriety. When special services are required, the counseling network makes referrals to appropriate services.

The judicatory person most likely to know that Jonathan or another church worker or family member is in need of counseling is the district superintendent, who functions somewhat like a bishop *in locus*. The district superintendent might recommend a specific counselor to Jonathan, however, the Florida Conference makes it possible for persons to secure counseling services confidentially, without the knowledge of the district superintendent.

Since complete confidentiality is possible, job security or future mobility are not obstacles to seeking counseling. The eighty percent preferred provider network coverage also reduces economic hardship and makes counseling more accessible.

Primary concerns that Florida Conference ministers and their families bring to counseling include marital and family stresses, particularly those related to frequent moves. With 700 churches in the Florida Conference, there are approximately 165 moves a year. One peak stress period is right after moves are announced.

The 1991 network counselor summary indicated 375 persons received counseling through the counseling network. The network counselors identified adjustment disorder as the most frequently presented problem, with marital problems second and depression third. While the divorce rate in the Florida Conference is still low, it is higher than it used to be. In the past, the Florida Conference had a "Conference Counselor" located in the conference offices. The present system of network counselors overcomes the necessity of a person going to the administrative center for counseling, further ensuring confidentiality. Currently there are forty-six counselors in the counseling network.

The counseling network does not provide continuing education, but programs designed to help prevent future problems are available through the Board of Ordained Ministry and in the local district. If Jonathan were a UMC pastor, he would be required to complete two credits of continuing education each year.

The districts provide programs on stress management, marital communication, family concerns, congregational conflict management, team ministry relationships, and vocational and spiritual development. Jonathan would have the opportunity to participate in such a preventive program every two to four years. In addition, the Florida Conference offers an annual spouse retreat. Congregations are asked to finance these continuing education programs.

As a new UMC minister, Jonathan would very quickly get acquainted with the congregation's Pastor-Parish Relations (or Pastor-Staff-Parish Relations) Committee. This very significant committee, required by UMC polity, interfaces with the district superintendent and/or the Bishop. While the committee cannot meet without the knowledge of the pastor, and while it cannot "vote out" a pastor, the Pastor-Parish Committee is an important voice in the process of pastoral selection and mobility. Membership on the committee is determined by a nominating committee, of which the pastor is the chair.

Outside the congregation, clergy participation in denomination peer support groups and ecumenical clergy groups is highly recommended. Not all pastors attend a clergy group, for reasons similar to professional leaders in other religious bodies: time limitations, no feeling of need, discomfort sharing at a more personal level, and the desire to maintain the appearance that everything is going well.

UMC Pastoral Care and Counseling Program

Another model for leadership support in the United Methodist Church is the Pastoral Care and Counseling program offered in central and southern Illinois. The Board of Ordained Ministry supports a full-time director who coordinates a support program for the personal care and counseling of professional leaders, spouses, and other family members. Services are provided without cost to the professional leader. The director is available for telephone and personal consultation and also coordinates referrals to other counseling resources, including Masters level psychologists, AAPC Diplomate Pastoral Counselors, and others.

While the director is a full-time staff person, the Pastoral Care and

Counseling program is completely confidential, and there is no contact with bishops or district superintendents unless such communication is spelled out by mutual contract of the judicatory, the client and the counselor. Confidentiality is a major concern of professional leaders and is carefully respected in the program. Counseling program activities are reported to the judicatory by aggregate data, not by specific instance (except with the informed consent of the counselee).

If Joan were a minister in central or southern Illinois, she could take advantage of the services of the Conference Pastoral Care and Counseling support program, but she would have other options as well. Through the conference insurance program, mental health coverage is available for problems that have a psychiatric diagnosis, although not for marriage counseling. Licensed psychiatrists, licensed psychologists, and AAPC Pastoral Counselors are accepted as providers under the insurance provisions.

Along with the counselor resources, the Pastoral Care and Counseling program offers a full complement of continuing education opportunities that serve as preventive programs. Within the conference Joan would be able to attend workshops on personal stress management and self-care, marriage, sexual ethics in ministry, chemical health issues, vocational concerns, and spiritual growth.

The Pastoral Care and Counseling program has developed a number of unique approaches to leadership support or made innovative adaptations of programs other judicatories have found helpful. For example, there are transition workshops for relocating pastors and spouses. A climate is established where it is safe to share feelings about the highs and lows of the recent move—what it is like for a single woman to arrive in town by herself with a U-Haul®, or what happens when a clergy couple learns on moving day that the new parsonage won't accommodate two rooms of their furniture! Joys and sorrows are kept in tension and there is a lot of permission to tell it like it is. The hope is that people will leave the transition workshop with some relief for having ventilated feelings and will have found some new persons for their support systems.

Other programmatic offerings are available for those in their middle years and at pre-retirement. One popular program is on men's issues. A ministry of memos communicates such suggestions as how to take a mini-vacation even if on a tight budget.

One final, distinctive feature of the Pastoral Care and Counseling program is the coordinator's availability by telephone each morning from

8:00 to 10:00 a.m. If Joan had something on her mind, whether a personal or a professional concern, she could telephone the coordinator between those hours and receive counsel by telephone.

The Florida Conference and the central and southern Illinois area of the United Methodist Church provide only two examples of UMC support. Though different in important respects, each reflects the values of the denomination at large.

14. Presbyterian Church (USA)

The Presbyterian Church (USA) has differences in approach at the regional level, but there is national coordination of a confidential counseling support program for the denomination's professional leaders and their families. The self-insurance program is provided by the denomination's Board of Pensions. Were Joan a Presbyterian pastor seeking counseling, she would pay twenty percent of the cost after a deductible of 1.5 percent of her annual cash salary plus the value of her housing (the deductible is higher if additional members of the family are receiving services). Like many other programs, this one requires that the problem fall within the category of a psychiatric diagnosis, therefore marriage, career, and vocational counseling are not covered.

Under the managed care program, any service Joan was to receive would need to be precertified. Counselors must be licensed or certified in their field and must accept the standard fee schedule. Psychiatrists, psychologists, social workers, AAPC Diplomate and Fellow pastoral counselors, marriage and family counselors, and psychiatric nurse specialists all may be approved if they meet the guidelines of the managed care program. When Joan called the managed care program, she would be given a referral to an appropriate service provider in her area; church professionals in remote rural areas have fewer resources from which to choose.

Joan's confidentiality is assured. She would select a counselor from a list of approved counselors and thereafter would have a confidential relationship with the counselor.

One difference between presbyteries is the focus of their continuing preventive education programs. Workshops in such areas as self-care, stress management, marriage and family, chemical health, conflict management, team ministries, vocational development, and spiritual growth are common. Workshops on sexual ethics were offered at the regional level in 1992, and some programs were presented at the presbytery level.

The national church encourages professional leaders to participate in peer support groups and congregational leader-layperson support committees; however, not all presbyteries reinforce this suggestion.

Other variations among the presbyteries were evident in their responses to the *Caring for the Caregiver* survey. For example, some presbyteries have a staff "Pastor to Pastors" and designated resources for career development and outplacement. When career counseling is offered, the professional leader may be asked to cover a substantial part of the costs; some presbyteries are able to assist in paying the costs of these services, others are not. Some presbyteries offer preventive programs in substance abuse and sexual misconduct. In some presbyteries, individual staff members provide support to professional leaders and/or subgroups of presbytery leaders through a regular program of visiting. In other areas there are mentoring programs for those entering ministry and orientations for professional leaders new to the area.

Despite these differences at the presbytery level, the presence of a nationally coordinated counseling support program represents a substantial commitment to leadership support. The variations at the presbytery level seem to reflect regional and local emphases as well as presbytery leadership priorities.

15. Reformed Church in America

If Jonathan were a pastor of The Reformed Church in America (RCA), he would have access to a denominational Clergy Support Service. He or any member of his family might be referred for confidential counseling to a psychiatrist, a doctoral level psychologist, a social worker, an AAPC Pastoral Counselor, or a marriage and family counselor. Through the cooperation of the regional and national church bodies, Jonathan could also receive career counseling at designated Career Counseling Development Centers, where outplacement services are also available.

Jonathan would have the opportunity to attend educational programs in the areas of self-care, sexual ethics, substance abuse, conflict manage-

ment, and spirituality. He would be encouraged to belong to denominational and interdenominational collegial support groups. RCA also sees
the value of congregational "mutual ministry" leader-layperson committees, but these are not available in every congregation.

Jonathan would also have the support of a rather innovative approach of the RCA. This approach is based on the assumption that every
member of the church, including pastors and their families, has the right
to pastoral care. With pastors and their families, however, the church
found that attempting to mix the administrative role of judicatory leader
with the pastoral care role was not effective.

As an alternative, the Office of Human Resources has designed a
model of care that utilizes retired pastors who are out of the competitive
network. The position description for these "pastors to pastors" forbids
them to comment negatively on any decision affecting the life of someone in their care. The retired pastor's wife is also a part of the pastoral
care team. Each receives a part-time stipend from the RCA Board of
Pensions for this work.

Each retired couple serves from forty to sixty clergy families. If
Jonathan and his wife were one of the families in their area, the retired
staff couple would make a confidential visit to them in their parish at least
once a year.

During their visit, the retired couple would check to see how things
were going with the Jonathan and his family. Trained to listen carefully,
the couple would be alert to the particular dynamics of the family and
their greatest joys and frustrations in ministry. They would talk about
new continuing educational opportunities or other services available
through the denomination and do whatever else they could to establish
trust and a mentoring friendship.

If it appeared that there were issues that would benefit from professional attention, the pastoral care team might suggest a referral to a local
resource. Confidentiality is assured, so Jonathan and his family can
develop an open relationship with the retired couple. Only systemic
issues are discussed with the Office of Human Resources, with no reference to individual situations.

Some issues that seem to affect many persons in ministry are the
stresses associated with mobility, including the parsonage system, un-
realistic role expectations, and family concerns (teenagers, grandchil-
dren, divorce, etc.). After starting the program, the experience of the
Reformed Church in America has been very positive and many wish that

this particular program of pastoral support had been implemented even earlier.

16. Roman Catholic

In the United States, the Roman Catholic Church is divided into regions, provinces, and dioceses. Each diocese is headed by a bishop. While there is a National Conference of Catholic Bishops, there is no national program for counseling support of professional leaders. Each diocese provides its own form of support, with the freedom to care for its caregivers in its own way. Because of this diocesan autonomy, it is necessary to look at the way individual dioceses approach leadership support.

In recent years, most dioceses have established an office for clergy personnel. Often it is called the Office of the Vicar for Priests. The Diocese of Orlando has a program that is fairly typical of those found elsewhere in the country. One of seven dioceses in Florida, Orlando has a Vicar General, a Vicar General Chancellor, and a Vicar for Priests. The Diocese of Orlando refers to the latter as the Office of Ministry to Priests.

If Jonathan were a priest in Orlando and he ran into some problems, he could speak directly to his brother priest who directs the Office of Ministry to Priests. This office then does its best to respond in a helpful way. John's consultation with the director of the Office of Ministry to Priests may or may not remain confidential, depending upon the situation. The Bishop is informed if there is the possibility that a priest's problem will become known to others.

Jonathan could chose to have a spiritual director or take advantage of one of the community counselors known to be helpful to priests. All or most of the cost of any counseling services, both outpatient and residential, would be covered by a commercial insurance program, and the Clergy Benevolent Fund or parish funds might also help if needed. If specialized care for alcoholism, sexual problems, or a comprehensive psychodiagnostic evaluation were needed, there are national church-related facilities to which a priest can be referred.

Each fall Jonathan would be able to go to a Priests' Convocation. The diocese also offers continuing educational programs on stress management, self-care, sexual issues and the priestly vocation.

The diocese has no specific provisions for career counseling. The priests have job security and reasonable mobility around the diocese. A survey of priests ordained from five to nine years indicated that those new priests who had field training and a mentoring program felt better prepared for their first parish assignment (Orlando was one of the dioceses sampled in a study supported by the Lilly Endowment and published by the Seminary Department of the National Catholic Educational Association.)

Of course, no one diocese gives an adequate picture of professional leadership support in the Roman Catholic Church. There are differences and commonalities between dioceses. Among those commonalities is access to Roman Catholic resources outside the particular diocese.

National Roman Catholic Resources

Although counseling support is not nationally coordinated, there are a number of national resources that support priests and other professional leaders. Some of these resources include the National Organization of Continuing Education of Roman Catholic Clergy (NOCERCC), the National Federation of Priests Councils (NFPC), the Conference of Major Superiors of Men (CMSM), the Leadership Conference of Women Religious (LCWR), and the National Association of Church Personnel Administrators (NACPA).

Most of the dioceses across the country belong to NOCERCC, whose mission is the formation and continuing education of clergy. NOCERCC's annual convention may bring together as many as 200 members from various dioceses and religious communities. Those who attend are the people involved in the continuing formation of Roman Catholic clergy. A recent convention theme was the meaning of an embodied priesthood, focusing on the physical dimension of humanness, including sexuality and celibacy. Convention programs can be replicated at the local level.

NOCERCC serves as a sort of clearinghouse for continuing education or formation opportunities. While not nationally coordinated, there are many universities, individual retreat houses, and religious communities that offer different kinds of programs throughout the country. NOCERCC compiles as much of this information as possible, with one recent listing of programs offered during a single summer filling twenty-nine pages! NOCERCC sent a copy of this listing to each member who in turn could copy the list for further publication.

In this and other ways, NOCERCC shares resources and provides material for dioceses to think through their local continuing formation needs. NOCERCC also publishes a booklet on sabbaticals, and professional leaders are encouraged to consider taking advantage of full-year or half-year sabbatical programs.

Whereas NOCERCC is an organization for priests, the membership of the National Association of Church Personnel Administrators (NACPA) includes many women leaders. At its annual meeting, NACPA publishes listings of support and sabbatical programs.

Another resource for leadership support is the National Federation of Priests Councils (NFPC). As a result of Vatican II, NFPC is structured in the same way as the National Conference of Catholic Bishops, giving priests a means for communication and representation with their bishops as they look together at the life of the diocese and the priestly life. NFPC is concerned with ways that priests can be helpful to their brother priests and publishes documents reviewing problems and offering helpful suggestions.

There is also a Conference of Major Superiors of Men (CMSM) which is composed of the provincials in charge of the various provinces of religious communities, such as the Jesuits, Franciscans, Dominicans, Augustinians, Brazilian Fathers, Benedictines, and Carmelites. The Conference assists provincials in offering support to the professional leaders within their communities. Burnout, leadership support, and mutually supportive life-styles are some of the topics considered. Retreats and sabbaticals are encouraged. There is also a leadership program for new provincials.

Women religious have an analogous group, the Leadership Conference of Women Religious (LCWR) for provincial leaders of the Sisters of Mercy, Sisters of Notre Dame, etc. The women religious have been very proactive.

Other offices, such as the National Association of Permanent Deacon Directors, address similar concerns as CMSM and LCWR, except for the permanent diaconate (deacons are ordained clergy, but not priests).

Through these various associations and groups, along with care and counseling that is available at the diocesan level, there is an effort in the Roman Catholic Church to meet as many of the basic support needs of priests and others in religious life as possible. The National Conference of Catholic Bishops meets as an entire body at least once or twice a year. The Bishops' Committee on Priestly Life and Ministry has a mission "to provide leadership regarding priestly ministry and to respond to the needs and concerns of priests. The Committee develops documents and other courses of action by which bishops support and challenge the life and ministry of priests."

The Secretariat for Priestly Life and Ministry of the National Conference of Catholic Bishops (see Appendix II) has a special concern for the well-being of professional leaders and keeps current on what is being done throughout the church to meet their needs. The Secretariat assists the Bishops' Committee in the fulfilling of its purpose "by doing research and developing drafts regarding the Committee's projects, by implementing the Committee's decisions, by developing communication about the Committee's activities, and by being available for consultation with individual dioceses and religious institutes."

A review of all of the religious bodies in this chapter suggests that there are not only differences, but also commonalities among the various denominations and religious groups. To take a look at some of those commonalities, let us now consider professional leadership support from the perspective of the different levels or types of support.

CHAPTER IV

Types of Support

The *Caring for the Caregiver* study identified different ways that religious bodies support professional leaders. As indicated earlier, the Lilly-supported study was not evaluative, and there were no assumptions about the greater value of any one form of support. However, there was a critical assumption that every religious group can learn from the experience and practices of other denominations or faiths.

In fact, most religious bodies share similar concerns. Some obvious exceptions exist. For example, celibate clergy do not have the marital pressures that married clergy do. But, in most respects, the similarities among professional leaders far surpass any differences. This is understandable since a person in ministry is first a *person*. Our personhood precedes any role we are subsequently trained to fill. Basic human problems are likely to affect persons like Joan or Jonathan without regard to the particular religious bodies in which they are ordained or certified.

As *persons* in ministry Jonathan and Joan will have common problems, but how Joan and Jonathan will be supported in their time of need will differ depending on the ecclesiastical polity of their particular religious body. For example, Jonathan may receive pastoral care from a retired pastor on a stipend because the Reformed Church in America has a national office to coordinate the program and a denominational Board of Pensions to provide the stipend. On the other hand, local autonomy may in some situations allow for increased flexibility and personalization of support.

Whatever the polity, in the various denominations and religious groups studied there are different levels of support, each of which has its own strengths and limitations. Those levels are:

    Personal
    Familial
    Congregational
    Collegial
    Community
    Denominational
    Interdenominational

Without implying a hierarchy of value and without reference to individual religious bodies, let us summarize what we have learned about the types of support available at these different levels and offer a few additional observations.

Personal

Every judicatory recognizes that professional religious leaders need support. Every religious body acknowledges that professional leaders sometimes experience stress, frustration, depression, burnout, second thoughts about vocational choice, and spiritual crises. No religious group in the survey simply wrote off these personal problems as failures of faith. Rather, these human problems are considered legitimate needs that judicatories should address as effectively as possible.

The sections that follow take another look at the primary areas of personal need and the principal ways that persons in ministry are currently being supported.

Familial

Those religious bodies that have a married clergy are increasingly aware of the need to provide care for both the professional leader and the spouse. Family life in a congregational context has singular dynamics that have been especially well described by Edwin Friedman, William Hulme, Robert Randall, Peter Steinke, and Lyndon Whybrew. Few, if any, other vocations make the demands on families that ministry does. Even though many spouses today have careers of their own and may not be completely involved in congregational life, the expectations and demands go beyond what they are for spouses of physicians, lawyers, psychologists, teachers, or other professionals.

Some religious bodies have found success in starting to work with couples during seminary. Special support is needed during the first few years in ministry. By establishing the support system during the seminary years, future problems sometimes can be prevented. Positive feedback from participants has led some denominations to make a permanent commitment to these programs.

Continuing education can serve a preventive purpose, and some denominations include spouses in the programs. Scheduling becomes a major challenge when spouses are included; child care concerns and the harried schedules of two-career couples make it difficult to carve out time for continuing education, no matter how worthwhile it may be. It can also be a challenge to promote support programs in an appropriate manner. Couples will not attend a program if they feel that by doing so they are sending a signal that there is trouble on the homefront. Think about it. Would a couple experiencing difficulties be more likely to attend a workshop entitled, "When Your Marriage Is in Trouble: Alternatives to Divorce," or one entitled "How Today's Love Can Last Through the Years?"

Those religious bodies that make personal visits just to see how things are going report a positive reception. However, if a pastor and spouse perceive that the visit has been prompted by a report that they are having marital problems, or if they believe the conversation will not be kept confidential, such a pastoral visit could feel quite threatening. It is questionable whether or not a judicatory official is the most helpful visitor unless a great deal of trust has previously been established.

In most of the religious bodies included in the study, spouses and family members have access to the same counseling support services that are provided for professional leaders. Most services are confidential and are covered in part by insurance. There is however a glaring omission on the part of a number of benefit programs in the exclusion of marriage and family counseling as a covered service. A number of the counseling programs require a psychiatric diagnosis before benefits are provided. One might question the wisdom of requiring a family situation to get so bad that a family member must become ill in order to receive insurance coverage for the costs of counseling. While some local judicatories may assist with some of the uncovered expenses, requesting assistance requires a family to compromise the confidentiality of both their financial situation and their family dynamics. The more systemic issue is that a religious body may convey a negative message to professional leaders and their families when marriage and family counseling support is specifically excluded from insurance coverage. While the purpose of the exclusion is to contain insurance costs, the exclusion may be interpreted as the failure of the church to be sensitive to the unique demands religious leadership places on marriage and family life.

Congregational

Not all religious groups have congregationally based "mutual ministry" committees. However, most denominations endorse the concept of a pastor-parish or a leader-lay staff support committee and hope to develop such a resource in the future.

Exactly what is meant by a mutual ministry committee depends on its formation and mission. There are several possibilities. Some staff support committees function as a personnel committee, representing the congregation. Issues of call, salary and benefits, responsibility and accountability are all appropriate issues for a personnel committee.

Or a committee may be a small representative group that interprets the concerns of the laity to the professional leader. This type of committee can be helpful to a professional leader by clarifying staff and congregational issues or conflicts and by suggesting alternative responses.

Either a personnel committee or a representative committee may be supportive to a professional leader, but the nature of the support may have some limitations. Both personnel and representative committees differ from another type of staff support committee that has as a primary purpose the personal support of the pastor and/or staff members.

One can often discern the true mission of a mutual ministry committee by examining how the committee members are selected. Are the members appointed by someone other than the professional leader or without the final approval of the professional leader?

The appointment of a person confers a certain responsibility. If the church council or church board appoints a committee member, is that committee member primarily accountable to the council or board? If the mutual ministry committee is accountable to another group, the professional leader may be reluctant to share personal information. Open communication with a mutual ministry committee is highly unlikely if confidentiality is not protected.

It is important to realize that personnel committees, representative committees, and personal support committees have their limits. Those professional leaders who try to use a mutual ministry committee as a substitute for personal counseling or therapy are asking the group to perform beyond its competency. If the primary purpose of the committee is personal support, it is more appropriate for the committee to stick with information, clarification, and, when appropriate, suggestion of viable alternatives. If professional therapy is needed, it is wiser for a staff support committee to encourage the professional leader to seek private and confidential support services outside of the congregation. It is also more pastoral for a professional leader to seek help outside of the congregation because the professional leader may be perceived as less available to respond to pastoral requests from a member or a committee that is trying to counsel or otherwise take care of the caregiver.

Staff support committees can be extremely helpful when organized thoughtfully and when expectations and limits are clearly outlined. The majority of those who have implemented such committees want to continue them; of those religious bodies that do not now have such committees, many seem to be interested in developing them. Different denominations may have written guidelines for developing staff support committees. One such guideline is that of the Evangelical Lutheran Church in America (see Appendix III).

Collegial

Most religious bodies seem to encourage their professional leaders to participate in denominational or ecumenical peer support groups. Many judicatory personnel indicate that collegial groups are essential to professional leadership support.

There seem to be a number of reasons why some professional leaders do not attend such groups. Respondents to the *Caring for the Caregiver* survey cited reasons ranging from time limitations, to no feeling of need for such a group, to the need to maintain the appearance of everything going well. The most common reason for non-attendance cited on the survey was "fear or distrust of sharing at a more personal level."

Colleagues in ministry sometimes create peer support by gathering around a task, perhaps a Bible study or a community concern. Considerable personal sharing may occur while the group works toward its goal. The stated agenda of the group is the task; the implicit agenda may be the support that comes from being together.

In *How To Build a Support System for Your Ministry*, Roy Oswald has described very well the pluses and minuses of collegial groups. He suggests that the most effective collegial groups do not simply happen by chance. Support groups are the result of very intentional decisions on the part of the participants. Oswald recommends that a group seek an outside leader. Leaderless groups seem much less helpful, and having someone within the group assume leadership often is counterproductive. Oswald provides a rationale for an outside leader and guidelines for starting a collegial group.

Special collegial groups are being developed by some denominations to provide support in particular circumstances of need. For example, a number of denominations recognize the importance of assisting the newly ordained in making healthy transitions into the professional ministry. Judicatories are identifying ways to provide the needed support and avoid the early burnout of persons with gifts for ministry. *Beyond the Boundary* (The Alban Institute, 1986) describes the different ways in which Episcopalians, Methodists, Presbyterians, and several Lutheran bodies provide support for seminarians entering full-time parish ministry. One of those approaches, the Pastoral Colleague Program, is currently being expanded from an earlier pilot program to wider implementation, utilizing interdenominational resources, and may be of interest to other religious bodies (see Apppendix II).

Community

Most of the religious bodies allow for the use of community resources when professional leaders or their families are in need of counseling support. In some denominations, the choice of a counselor is entirely a matter of personal choice.

Confidentiality is a concern of all professional leaders. Those denominations that rely on counselors or counseling networks selected by the denomination have to make special efforts to assure professional leaders that the use of those resources is truly confidential.

Where do persons in ministry go for help? Most have physicians for physical problems, but when personal or family counseling resources are needed, there may be some hesitation to use them. Some persons in ministry and their families are comfortable utilizing the same community counseling resources to which they might refer parishioners. Others are not. This visibility may be even more of a concern in smaller towns or places with fewer options for specialized care.

There are several factors to consider when professional leaders are trying to find the right place to go for help. Byers, McLaughlin, and Casto of the Ohio State University Commission on Interprofessional Education and Practice have noted five "A's" that are significant criteria for any type of health care. Quality health care is:

1. Available
2. Accessible
3. Affordable
4. Accountable
5. Affable

Care, regardless of its quality, is not a resource if it is not available and accessible. If unaffordable, treatment may be avoided or it will end too soon. Accountability suggests that resources must fulfill their promise to deliver services, and affability indicates the desirable climate of mutual trust that is needed in a helping relationship.

There are two other A's that are critical for persons in ministry and their families to consider. Quality care also must be:

6. Appropriate and
7. Adequate

"Appropriateness" and "adequacy" need further definition. It is *appropriate* for a physician to evaluate a headache and to prescribe the best available treatment, which may in some cases be pain medication. However, if a patient continues to report headaches after it has been determined that there is no physical cause for them, then it is no longer *adequate* to simply prescribe pain medication. When the patient is regarded as a whole person, the headache may be a signal that another part of the person's life is crying out for relief.

Furthermore, professional leaders and their families require counseling resources that understand not only the interrelatedness of life and how our physical nature interracts with how we think and feel and relate, but also the way in which all the dimensions of our humanness are integrated spiritually.

Denominational

Of the religious bodies surveyed, most are attempting to provide resources to meet the diverse needs of professional leaders and their families. Nonetheless, there is considerable variation in what is provided— nationally coordinated programs, combinations of national and regional programs, regional programs, and no coordinated programs.

Who provides the counseling? In some religious groups, there may be a staff person who is the designated counselor. That counselor may be part of the judicatory staff, or may be a pastoral counselor who has no authority over the professional leaders who are counseled. The religious body may provide a list or network of counselors. Or professional leaders may be allowed to choose any counselor.

However, insurance concerns may greatly affect the choice of a counselor. For example, psychiatrists and doctoral level psychologists usually meet insurance requirements, but in some denominations pastoral counselors or Masters level counselors may not be eligible unless they are under direct supervision. Also, in some denominational programs the services of privately selected counselors are not reimbursed at the same level as those counselors pre-approved by the religious body.

The *Caring for the Caregiver* survey compared the support programs of the various religious bodies along the following dimensions with the following results:

1. *Coordination*: national, regional, dioceses, presbyteries, districts, conferences, synods, etc., or no coordination at all. Examples of all of these were found.

2. *Coverage*: commercial insurance program, religious body's self-insurance program, or none. Most common were self-insurance programs, with some using commercial insurance in whole or as a supplement.

3. *Counselors*: which disciplines are recognized? Psychiatrists and psychologists were recognized by all, pastoral counselors, social workers, and marriage and family counselors by many, and career counselors by some.

4. *Confidentiality*: is it possible for professional leaders and their families to seek out *confidential* care and counseling? The answer was always "Yes."

5. *Comprehensiveness*: are all kinds of counseling needs supported or only those with a psychiatric diagnosis? Psychiatric disorders were covered by all insurance programs, but marriage counseling was not always covered and career counseling typically was not. Though not covered by insurance, usually career counseling was financially supported at least in part by the religious body.

6. *Counseling Specializations*: does the religious body have or recommend specific national or regional counseling programs for specific difficulties, such as substance abuse, sexual misconduct, financial impropriety? There were very few specialized resources identified. Most religious groups seemed to refer persons with these types of problems to the same resources used for other problems.

7. *Concern and Concerns*: to what extent should a judicatory head make personal contact with a professional leader to discuss any concerns that a professional leader might have about the consequences of entering a counseling program? There was no unanimity in responses to this question. A number felt such contact prior to the referral was desirable, and perhaps afterward, but most did not think that such contact would be appropriate while the professional leader was in treatment.

8. *Choices*: which approach to care and counseling is emphasized? As noted above, some utilize a staff person, some a network of counselors, and some emphasize the professional leader making that selection personally and privately.

9. *Continuing Education*: what kinds of programs designed to prevent future problems are offered? The most common were personal self-care, stress management, and spirituality. Marriage enrichment and congregational issues (conflict management, leadership style, etc.) were also fairly common offerings. The majority of those surveyed are doing something in the area of sexual ethics in ministry and chemical health issues. Usually these programs are offered every one to two years, and spouses often are invited to attend. Among professional leaders who do not attend these programs, there are several common reasons for non-participation: distance, cost, no personal need, and fears that attending would signal the existence of a problem. Occasionally, poor quality programs were cited as a deterrent.

10. Care in Context: what kinds of support groups does the religious body encourage professional leaders to attend? Most recommended denominational or ecumenical peer support groups, as well as congregational "mutual ministry" support committees. Reasons why professional leaders might not be involved in such groups included time limitations, no awareness of a need for such a group or committee, fear or distrust of sharing at a more personal level, and the need to maintain the appearance of everything going well.

11. Concluding Comments: what forms of professional leadership support are considered essential for a religious body to have in place if a professional leader is to feel supported? Almost all religious bodies said counseling/therapy and preventive continuing education were essential. Peer support groups and congregational mutual ministry committees were also frequently identified as essential components of a support program.

At the judicatory level, the commonalities among the religious bodies far outweigh the dissimilarities. The commitment to the support of professional leaders and their families is not greater in one religious body than in the others. As we have seen, differences are most often related to polity or to the limitations of insurance coverage.

Interdenominational

The majority of religious bodies have their own approach to professional leadership support and the development of denominational resources. However, any given denomination may call upon resources that are also used by other denominations.

A primary example of inter-denominational cooperation is the reliance on career counseling development centers. Many denominations include an ecumenical career counseling center among their resources. Candidacy evaluations are sometimes completed at career counseling centers and a number are now offering outplacement services as well as supportive services to experienced leaders.

Different denominations tend to share common counselor networks. The primary criteria for counselors are competency in counseling and sensitivity to faith issues. Most denominations do not require that the counselor be a member of the same denomination as the professional leader who is receiving counseling.

In the recent past, a number of ecumenical centers have been developed. Some began as denominational resources, but then became ecumenical in outlook and marketing. Appendix III lists a number of ecumenical centers that have been used by different denominations for inpatient treatment. The advantage of ecumenical centers for intensive and extensive care is just that: problems can receive focused attention for as long as is needed. The disadvantages include increasing questions insurance companies raise about the costs of extended programs and the uprooting from a person's home locality that such programs require. Sometimes being out of the home environment is therapeutically helpful; sometimes it is not.

There are many types of support. The personal and familial types typically support the *person* in ministry, with the focus on the human dimensions of the problem. Congregational and collegial support assist the person in *ministry*, where personal support may be important but the accent is more often on strengthening the professional capacities of the minister. Religious bodies seem to share a commitment to draw upon denominational, community, and ecumenical resources in an effort to provide what professional leaders and their families need in order to be as effective as possible in personal and vocational life.

The types of support we have discussed in this chapter represent the commitment of religious bodies to leadership support and the approaches to support that are generally taken or encouraged. The reality, of course, is that each professional leader and family member represents a particular, personal challenge for support. Therefore, we now turn to examine how individual differences affect support programs.

CHAPTER V

The Whens and Hows of Support

Differences between people—in life history, in present ministry context, and in personality—make a tremendous difference in the nature of the support that is appropriate and adequate. What follows are some illustrations of how these differences play out in reality, and some suggestions about the "whens and hows" of support. While the list of situations and support possibilities is not exhaustive, the suggested approaches can be adapted to a variety of situations. Because we already have discussed some of the special support needs of those who are married, the following sections will be devoted to other special life or vocational circumstances.

First we'll look at support needs that arise even in the best of times. Then we'll take some of the support perspectives that apply to the good times and see what happens when the times are not so good. But first, the good times.

In Good Times

In contrast to thirty years ago, in many denominations one half or more of those who now come to seminary today are married. Of course, that statistic also means that many seminarians are single (more than one-half if we include those preparing for Roman Catholic priesthood or other holy orders!) Many of these seminarians enter ministry as single persons.

Pastors Jonathan and Joan, whom we met earlier, were single when they entered seminary. Jonathan had been a public school teacher before seminary; Joan had come to seminary straight from college.

In personality, Jonathan and Joan are quite different. Joan enjoys people and values warm, friendly relationships. She is generally accepting and trustful. On the Myers-Briggs Type Indicator, Joan comes out ESFJ. The "E" at the beginning of ESFJ means "Extravert," or one who gets energy from the outside world, as in interaction with other people. The S means Sensing, or one who "sees" with the senses (sight, sound, smell, taste, touch). The F means one who makes decisions with Feeling judgment, which has as the "bottom line" person-centered values, harmony, and decisions that maintain or create good relationships. The final letter, J, means Judging—not judgmental, but rather one who prefers a lifestyle that is organized and orderly and appreciates closure. Joan likes to have life pretty much under control and when decisions need to be made, she is for making them and getting them out of the way.

Growing up Joan had some hard times. She was raised in a family that now would be called dysfunctional. Her father was a workaholic who seldom had time for Joan or the other children and her mother was a lonely person who sometimes would express her frustration and anger in no uncertain terms. Joan often was called upon to be the peacemaker or "fixer" in the home, but the peace rarely lasted for very long. The church represented some stability in her early life, so no one was surprised when Joan decided to go to seminary.

Unlike some of her classmates who had accepted staff ministry positions, Joan accepted a solo call to a community church where the previous pastor had resigned under the cloud of some possible sexual impropriety. Joan was the first female pastor ever called by the congregation and their expectations of her were very high, almost as high as Joan's expectations of herself! When she arrived, everyone seemed enthusiastic, happy, and eager to help.

Pastor Jonathan also had some hard times growing up, but for different reasons. His family was quite repressive. John's father rarely raised his voice or expressed emotion unless he had been drinking, when he could be very loud. John's mother was what now is called co-dependent. She covered for her husband, making excuses to his employer when he was unable to go to work because of his drinking. She also impressed on Jonathan the importance of good behavior, making clear-headed decisions and acting in a calm, controlled way. She took Jonathan to church where his religious training reinforced what he was being taught at home about "negative" feelings. Based on what he learned in church, not only was the expression of strong feelings a danger to rationality, but also to his soul.

In personality, Jonathan was quite different from Joan. His MBTI type came out INFP. The "I" means Introversion. Rather than getting his energy from the outside world, as Joan does, Jonathan is energized by the inner world of thoughts and ideas. While he uses his eyes and ears and other senses, his way of "seeing" is with N, which stands for Intuition. Jonathan relies on a kind of "sixth sense" about things when he takes in information. The "P" at the end of INFP stands for Perception, which means John's preferred lifestyle is not as organized and orderly as Joan's, but more open-ended and adaptable to whatever is going on at the time. When it comes to decision-making, Jonathan prefers not to come to closure too soon so that no options are inadvertently eliminated.

The one personality preference Jonathan shares with Joan is the "F," which stands for Feeling judgment. This may seem surprising since Jonathan was raised to be somewhat afraid of feelings. But Feeling judgment is not the same thing as making decisions based on feelings. Rather, Feeling judgment means a person prefers to come to a final decision on the basis of person-centered values that preserve harmony. It is a rational process, not an emotional one. While the majority of American males have a preference for Thinking judgment (decision-making based on an objective, logical analysis), the majority of men in most seminaries have a preference for making decisions based on Feeling judgment.

A second fact about John's INFP preference is that John's use of Feeling judgment is not as apparent as Joan's. Joan *extraverts* her Feeling judgment, which means that others are more aware of the person-centered way she goes about decision-making. Jonathan *introverts* his Feeling judgment, which means his reflection is internal, and others may not know the value he places on decisions that create harmony.

Support for Single Ministers

With this background about Jonathan and Joan, let's now take a look at some of the particular support needs of professional leaders who are single, needs that exist even when times are good.

One of the findings of the *Caring for the Caregiver* study was that support groups have the potential to be very helpful, whether they are

---

collegial, peer support groups or leader-layperson mutual ministry or staff support groups. The common denominator is that someone is there for the professional leader during what can, at times, be a very lonely vocation.

Both Jonathan and Joan lost the supportive network of friends and acquaintances they had in seminary when they moved to the parish; they lost their confidantes just at a time when they really could have used a sympathetic ear.

One of the great advantages of being married is that (ideally) you have a live-in partner to support and listen to you. Neither Joan nor Jonathan had that kind of built-in support system when they were in one of the most important transitional times of their lives.

Even though both of them experienced the loss of a supportive community, Joan and Jonathan felt that loss in very different ways. Joan had a great number of friends in the seminary since she was such a friendly and outgoing person herself. While her initial reception in the congregation was warm and welcoming, it did not take her long to recognize that the nature of her relationships with parishioners would be far different from those with her peers in seminary. She began to miss the less formal way of relating that she had known before.

On the other hand, Jonathan was quite a private person even when he was in seminary. He was never one to make a great many friends, but he did miss not having at least one person with whom he could be himself. This was especially true in those areas that touched on his personal values. Jonathan felt especially vulnerable about sharing his deepest feelings with anyone except a close friend, so he chose to hold in those feelings. But he began to have physical symptoms of stress.

From a judicatory standpoint, the time of transition into the parish is believed to be a joyful time of new beginnings. After all, seminary studies are over and seminarians are at last getting to do what they have waited so long to do!

Beginning ministry *is* a good time, but it is also a time when support is very much needed. Joan probably would benefit from one of her denomination's pastoral colleague groups for those just entering the parish. The group interaction appeals to most extraverts and is an excellent way to clarify thoughts and feelings and to get new ideas. At the same time, the group could help Joan rein in her tendency to be a Pastor Fixit—possibly a carry over from her early life.

Jonathan may find a colleague group helpful, but he might respond even more positively to a personal visit by someone in the judicatory or a personal visit by an experienced colleague. Introverts tend to prefer one-on-one communication and personal responses. Given John's history with his father, it would be important for the judicatory representative or pastoral colleague to be consistent and caring. Jonathan may at first be more comfortable talking about ideas than about feelings until a relationship of trust is established.

The importance of support in the good times should not be ignored. Parents know the importance of affirmation when things are going well —and if parents don't know it, surely their children do. A positive word from someone we respect can boost our self-esteem. Affirmation from our judicatory and colleagues means a lot more than most of us realize, and this is especially so for the seminarian making the transition into full-time ministry.

Special Challenges of Women in Ministry

Women in ministry have special challenges. Someone has made the insightful observation that when a male enters a new ministry context, competence is assumed but the congregation wonders if the minister will be caring. Congregations assume that a woman minister will be caring, but will she be competent? Obviously this is a generalization, but one which holds true in many congregations.

Some of the differences between how males and females in ministry are received by parishes is rooted in sexism; congregations need to grow out of this mindset, but how to do that is a matter of debate. Some believe that a sustained, positive experience with a woman minister will do more to overcome sexism than a frontal verbal or intellectual assault. People can be loved into changing, but forced changes rarely stick. On the other hand, people cannot have a positive experience with a woman minister unless she is present, and that may require some advocacy and intervention on the part of a judicatory.

Sexism, however, does not explain all the differences in the way males and females are received into a parish. Males and females have differing gifts and the goal is not that everyone be the same, but that the gifts of each are appreciated and affirmed.

Joan brings special personality gifts into her ministry. Her preferences for ESFJ are similar to those of many laywomen, which will
probably make it easier for them to relate to Joan than to someone (male
or female) with very different personality gifts. Her ES_J preferences
are also very similar to many laymen (remember, the Thinking preference is more common among males). Because she is action-oriented,
practical-minded, and organized, Joan will probably make a good first
impression. She may well be an example of one who will be easily
perceived as caring.

The question Joan will face will be that of competency. If a judicatory staff member or a colleague helps Joan to see how to include Thinking (T) judgment especially when she is working with her church board
or council, then the competency question will be short lived. As Feeling
types, both Joan and Jonathan will need to know how to speak the language of those who prefer Thinking (T) judgment. Initially, though, as a
woman Joan will need to be especially concious of using "T" or Thinking language in certain situations.

Joan faces several other challenges. Based on her personal history,
Joan may be especially sensitive to the normal upsets and conflicts that
occur in every congregational family. She also may be bothered by the
withdrawal or apparent indifference of laymen or the unexpected verbal
aggressiveness of laywomen. According to one way of understanding
personhood, we not only *have* a personal history, in a sense we *are* our
history. Knowing our history is important; seemingly innocent events
can trigger responses that originate deep in our childhood. As a woman,
Joan must also be cautious about sexist stereotypes that could be reinforced if she loses her cool and becomes "emotional."

An additional challenge comes out of the history of the congregation. Since there was a cloud of possible sexual impropriety hanging
over the departure of the previous pastor, Joan probably will be observed
very closely for her appropriateness in male-female relationships. Since
she is a single woman, that poses additional complications. The juxtapo-
sition of perceived availability with role inappropriateness can be a
heavy burden for a single woman to carry. The counsel and support of a
female judicatory representative or nearby female colleague could help
Joan meet this challenge.

There are other hurdles for women in ministry, even when the times
are good. Carefully listening to female colleagues in ministry is prob-

ably the best way to learn what they are. Some judicatories have been more intentional than others in the development of support for women in ministry. The efforts of the United Methodist Church and some of the publications of The Alban Institute do not stand alone, but they do represent concerted efforts to address the issues of women in ministry (see Books and References).

Challenges of Male Ministers

Jonathan faces his challenges, too. If competence is assumed but caring is not, Jonathan will need to show his warmth early in his ministry. Although an INFP is typically a caring person, since John's Feeling values are naturally introverted, he could be perceived as more reserved than caring. When it comes to decision making, his open-ended style may be mistaken for indecisiveness. Getting to know parishioners by making pastoral visits is a good way to be seen as both competent and caring, but it takes a lot of energy for an Introvert to do all that extraverting!

As a male, Jonathan probably will face fewer prejudices than a woman. But INFP personality preferences are not those of a stereotypical male, so Jonathan will benefit from support that helps him clarify the expectations of the congregation, particularly in relation to what the congregation expected of the male pastor who preceded Jonathan.

Judicatory and collegial support also needs to be tailored to John's personal life history. That may be difficult, because Jonathan may not be quick to talk about his developmental history with people who are not very close friends. Even with them, he may more easily share thoughts than feelings about the past.

Having an alcoholic father, Jonathan lived with the unpredictability children experience when they don't quite know how their alcoholic parent is going to behave on a given day. Since John's father became loud and emotional when he drank, Jonathan may unconciously shrivel a bit when dealing with loud persons whose emotions seem out of control. Jonathan may also be particularly sensitive to excuses for inappropriate behavior or for broken promises.

If a judicatory staff person or colleague wants to support Jonathan, reliability would be crucial—saying what is going to be done and doing it. The development of trust may take some time. Jonathan could also use some modeling in how to appropriately express feelings about what happens in parish ministry. He may well benefit from learning some assertiveness skills to help him manage his fears that any expression of feelings may get out of control. Rather than risk being aggressive, Jonathan may become passive-aggressive, expressing anger in indirect ways. Assertiveness training could help Jonathan establish appropriate boundaries around his strong feelings, helping him become a much more effective minister.

Common Issues for All Ministers

It is not true-to-life to make such clear divisions between female and male ministers. While there are some distinctions, such as the greater likelihood that women in ministry will be subjected to sexist attitudes and behaviors, there are also many commonalities. For example, personality type preferences cut across gender. A Feeling type male minister like Jonathan (person-centered valuing of interpersonal harmony) has things in common with a Feeling type female minister like Joan; Jonathan may not have as much in common with another male minister who is a Thinking type (logical, analytical, prizing principles more than harmony). Conversely, a female Thinking type minister may communicate more effectively with a Thinking type male minister than with a Feeling type like Joan, whose decision-making process is very different.

Similarities in personal life history or present ministry circumstances may also cut across gender lines. Both Jonathan and Joan know the meaning of a dysfunctional home. There is a difference between alcoholism and workaholism, but both Jonathan and Joan know what it is like to have parents who are emotionally unavailable to their children. Learning how to appropriately express feelings and assert oneself are tasks which apply to both females and males who have been raised in dysfunctional environments.

For both males and females in ministry, there are issues of the *person* in ministry—personality and personal life history—and of the person in *ministry*—the theological understanding of ministry and the role expectations of ministers in a particular ministry context. Where it is helpful to see these issues from the perspective of the gift of being female or male, then it is useful to do so. Where it is helpful to look beyond gender to the common concerns of persons in ministry, then it is wise to do that.

Issues of Multiple Staff Ministries

Rather than the solo ministries they entered, Joan or Jonathan could have become part of a staff ministry. If either had, their experience probably would have been different.

In part, that difference would have to do with gender. If Joan went to a congregation that never before had a female professional leader, then she would wrestle with the assumptions and expectations we discussed earlier. Joan's experience might be affected by whether or not she was appointed by the judicatory or elected by a congregational vote; dynamics are different when a minister is serving in a congregation by the congregation's choice.

Jonathan would face certain challenges if he entered a situation where there had never before been an assistant or associate minister. Congregations enter into a new staff arrangement with certain assumptions and expectations. How clearly those are communicated to a new staff member can make the difference between a smooth entry and a rocky one.

Apart from gender and the staffing pattern, there are other ways in which Jonathan and Joan would have different experiences in staff ministry, even in the best of situations. The key factor in staff ministry is the match that exists or that is developed between the persons on the staff. Though it is a limited analogy, the significance of the relationship of ministers who are serving a congregation parallels what ideally happens when a wife and husband have children. If the parents have and maintain a good, rounded, balanced, healthy relationship, the children are blessed. Their nurturing of each other overflows into the better nurturing of those who depend on them.

Matching in staff ministry means more than compatible personalities. Staff ministers can genuinely like each other as persons, but be seriously mismatched theologically or pastorally. They can also enjoy each other's company but differ in their preferred approach to worship, their understanding of what constitutes a responsible relationship to the judicatory, or their method of working with lay leadership. And the list goes on.

Values, priorities, content, and process differences are wisely explored prior to entering into a staff relationship. This exploration is essential pre-work before a minister is called or appointed, whether by judicatory or congregation.

While matching in staff ministry requires far more than compatibility of personalities, a good match also requires attention to personality dynamics. Because of personality differences, Joan and Jonathan would have different experiences in team ministry if they worked with the same senior pastor. Let's say the senior pastor, Patrick, had personality preferences of Extraversion (energy comes from and is directed to the outside world), Intuition (information gathering by looking beyond the data to patterns and possibilities), Thinking (objective, logical, analytical, and impersonal in the sense of not wanting feelings to bias decision making) and Judging (not judgmental, but a preference for organization and order). On the Myers-Briggs, Patrick's preferences would be ENTJ.

Even if their theological and ministerial priorities seemed to be compatible, eventually personality differences would come to the fore. With Joan, Patrick shares preferences for action (Extraversion) and organization (Judgment is the J at the end of both ESFJ and ENTJ). However, they most naturally will "see" different things. Joan's Sensing may notice more specific things about individual people, and how individual people are doing is likely to be very important to her (her Feeling preference). Patrick's Intuition may more easily pick up emerging patterns in the organizational system, and planning based on a more personal, unbiased logical analysis is one of Patrick's principles (his Thinking preference). It is not hard to see that, from time to time, Patrick and Joan would need to help each other understand why each goes about ministry differently, even though they might share the same theology and claim very similar overall goals for the congregation.

Were Patrick to be working with Jonathan, the fact that they are both males would not change the reality that, in personality, they have very significant differences. For example, Jonathan does not get energy from the outside world nor is he as naturally action-oriented as Patrick. As an Introvert, Jonathan is probably a reflective person who also likes to keep his options open (Perception, the P at the end of INFP). Jonathan is quite adaptable and comfortable going with the flow. Yet, to Patrick, this might make Jonathan appear disorganized and procrastinating. In addition, John's Feeling preference contrasts with Patrick's Thinking preference, just as Joan's did. Jonathan is most likely to view human impact as more important than systemic impact, quite the opposite of what Patrick prefers to do. Consequently, even though they might share a common vision for the future of the congregation, Patrick and Jonathan will need to work to keep their relationship free from misunderstandings and misinterpretations.

These are only a few of the implications of personality differences in staff ministry. Seminaries and judicatories can be more supportive if they recognize that many conflicts that arise in staff ministries result from differences in personality preferences. Those differences are not insurmountable. There are no inherently incompatible personality types in team ministry. The Myers-Briggs should never be used to screen out a potential staff member. Effective team ministry can take place in the midst of different personality types, if team members are a good match in theology and ministry priorities, and if they are at least theoretically committed to the idea that differing (complementary) personality preferences are good gifts from God.

When Times Are Bad

What does a professional leader do when he or she wearies along the way? Any person in ministry can get to the place where life, work, and even faith seem to have run into a dead end. The joy of ordination or certification once was real, but for some that joyful moment is only a memory. The sense of call can fade and the assurance that Christ will be with us always can seem like a promise meant for someone else.

In Conflict Situations

What we have just reviewed about conflicts that arise out of personality differences applies to virtually any conflict situation in a parish because personality differences are usually a factor. For example, the differences in perception and judgment between Patrick and Joan, or Patrick and Jonathan, would be as likely to occur if Joan or Jonathan were lay leaders. If Patrick (ENTJ) were a lay leader or questioning member of a congregation, what Patrick might "see" and say to Joan or Jonathan as pastors could well precipitate a conflict situation.

When the Congregational Family is Feuding

Over and over again in the *Caring for the Caregiver* study, judicatory leaders and parish ministers spoke of the toll that is taken by congregational infighting. Many of the referrals of professional leaders for counseling or vocational consultation arise out of stressful congregational conflicts. By the time the judicatory is called in (if it is), the situation may require a miracle if reconciliation is to occur. Stress, depression, burnout, and resignation from the ministry context or from the full-time ministry often are the result of intense conflicts that have spun out of control.

Family systems theory is very helpful in examining congregational conflicts. Most current professional leaders were not trained in family systems perspectives, but it is one of the most useful ways of looking at conflict. Judicatories can support professional leaders by having a staff member who has had basic training in family systems theory.

Family systems theory does not identify a "patient" or someone who is in the wrong or in the right. Instead, the focus is on how the system is working (or not working) and what it takes to transform a dysfunctional system into a functional one. The goal is not to win or lose. The whole congregation wins if the energy lost in infighting can be transformed into energy for ministry and mission.

One of the reasons the family systems model is so appropriate for congregations is that it takes history seriously—personal history as well as congregational history. The popular saying about the need of children for roots and wings applies also to a congregational family. Tradition and innovation in ministry are not necessarily contradictory, if we affirm the need for both roots and wings. When applied to the parish, family systems theory does not overlook the past. Nor does it suggest that we get stuck there. Rather, what is offered is a mature way of honoring a heritage while following a vision of the future into which God calls us.

When an understanding of personality differences is integrated with family systems theory we can create a growth model that I think is the best currently available for working with professional leaders in conflict situations. *God's Gifted People* provides a biblical basis for appreciating and affirming differences in personality as gifts from God rather than as thorns in the flesh. The work of Edwin Friedmann, Peter Steinke, and Lyndon Whybrew is very helpful in developing the ideas of family system theorist Murray Bowen and applying Bowen's ideas to congregational life.

Substance Abuse and Denial

Personality type and family systems theory also can help us understand another major area of concern, substance abuse.

The term substance abuse often conjures images of illegal street drugs. The *Caring for the Caregiver* survey suggested that for persons in ministry the drug of choice is alcohol.

Along with failing to recognize alcohol as a drug, professional religious leaders may also deny that alcohol is much of a problem among ministers. I once attended a community meeting on the topic of the impaired professional. The presentation panel included a physician, an attorney, and a clergyperson. The program began with a brief word from each of the leaders about "the problem." The physician stood up and said something like the following: "We physicians have a problem. Some of us are impaired by alcohol and some by other drugs that we prescribe for ourselves. Our patients suffer if we do not face this real need and so we are developing an impaired physician program for doctors."

The attorney was next. His words were close to these: "We attorneys also have a problem. Alcohol abuse, in particular, affects too many of us and our clients are affected by our abuse. We need to have an impaired attorney program available for those who recognize their problem and for those who aren't aware but can be referred when they need it."

The clergyperson was the last to speak. The assembled group expected something like what they had heard from the physician and the attorney. Instead, the clergyperson said, in essence, "We clergy have a problem. With increasing numbers of people sitting in our pews suffering from the effects of alcohol and drugs, how do we minister to them?"

Nobody in the audience laughed. The clergyperson was not trying to be funny. It was obvious that the point of the meeting had been missed. No matter how overused the defense mechanism of denial, *all* professionals are susceptible to impairment from the abuse of alcohol and other drugs, and that includes ministers!

Research on substance abuse indicates that no race or class or gender is immune to the potential for addiction. Persons with a family history of addiction may have a vulnerability associated with hereditary and environmental factors, but obviously not all persons with alcoholic parents or grandparents become alcoholics themselves. Furthermore, there are those who become addicted who have no known family members with addictive problems. If the research ever fully identifies predisposing factors, they will always remain only that—predispositions. There is neither safety nor inevitability if predispositions are unquestionably established.

At the same time, there is something that ministers can learn from the research on predisposing factors, whether hereditary or environmental. John's father was an alcoholic and Jonathan learned co-dependent behavior as a child.

With his heredity and history, Jonathan should be alert to warning signals. If he found himself thinking about or starting to take a drink at the end of a long, hard day or after a frustrating meeting, it would be crucial that he remember his father's drinking. Jonathan might believe that he knows when to stop drinking, even if his father didn't. Also, perhaps John's father drank in bars and Jonathan only drinks at home. These "differences" may obscure the presence of an addictive pattern. John's father started drinking to relieve tension and stress. If there is indeed a predisposing biochemistry, the progression from drinking to relieve stress to alcohol addiction will probably only be a matter of time.

If Jonathan were to develop a problem with alcohol, others might become aware of it before Jonathan. One of the managed mental health care companies, Biodyne, quotes a saying: "Garlic before onion." What it means is that if we eat onions, we may later have some indigestion— and we know it! But if we eat garlic, a few hours later we may feel great, but others will be saying "Phew!" Persons with problems like anxiety and phobias know full well that something is wrong, and they often seek help. Those suffering from alcoholism are more like those who eat garlic. They may not realize they have a problem even though others are sure they do. Whatever else stresses a minister, if alcohol is a problem it needs to be addressed before other personal or professional issues can be resolved.

Some institutions and persons have long been associated with an appropriate response to substance abuse, particularly alcoholism. Hazelden, the Menninger Foundation, and Parkside-Lutheran General Behavioral Health Corporation are just a few examples. The work of Jonathan Keller, Sharon Wegschieder, and Janet Woititz has also been influential in recent years (see Books and References).

Also, Jonathan should be mindful even if he himself decides never to use alcohol. It is a truism that one cannot become an alcoholic if one never takes a drink. But that would not necessarily "cure" John's family history. Even if Jonathan never drinks, he still carries the baggage of his early life. Jonathan may unconsciously approach his pastoral ministry in a co-dependent manner. Melody Beattie's book, *Co-dependent No More*, was passed around in caregiving circles because she struck a responsive cord in so many of those in helping professions.

Those who learned co-dependent behavior early in life are quick to pick up the signs of neediness in others, and they do their best to rescue those in need. What is not so apparent is that such helpers may be meeting their *own* needs more than they are actually helping someone else. They may have a special need to "save" someone now because they were so frustratingly unsuccessful in saving their parent (and themselves) while growing up.

One example of co-dependent behavior is to try to protect somebody with a problem from the consequences of his or her behavior. Jonathan would probably have observed his mother making excuses for his father, offering acceptable reasons for his father's absences or calling in to her husband's employer to cover when he failed to go to work. Even if Jonathan never takes a drink of alcohol, he will want to become aware of the way that co-dependency and ministry can get confused. He also will wisely remain alert to the way that the same dynamics could play in his marriage, family, and friendships. If Jonathan wanted to examine the impact of his early years, a helpful book for him (and his spouse) to read is Woititz's *Adult Children of Alcoholics*.

Jonathan is not the only one affected by dynamics arising out of a dysfunctional family of origin. Joan, too, knows something about the impact on family life of workaholism. While not an addicting substance like alcohol or other drugs, Woititz points out that many children other than those of alcoholics can recognize themselves in the Adult Children of Alcoholics (ACoA) descriptors. A similar message is given in *Recovery from Loss*, which explores the impact of early life experiences on how persons perceive and react to situations of change and loss.

Even in denominations where there is a strict prohibition against drinking, substances can be abused and the defense mechanism of denial can get in the way of opening oneself to help and recovery. In addition to those in the pew who need help, there needs to be an increased emphasis in seminaries on the use, misuse, and abuse of chemicals—and on what to do if we recognize signs of trouble in our colleagues and ourselves.

Is Nothing Sacred?

Is Nothing Sacred? is the title of Marie Fortune's book about what happens "when sex invades the pastoral relationship." Enormous damage takes place in the lives of individuals and congregations when the leader is involved in sexual impropriety. Concern about sexual misconduct was raised in almost all of the responses to the *Caring for the Caregiver* study.

Judicatories have attempted to be responsible in addressing these problems. For example, Fortune's book includes the guidelines developed by the Northwest District of the American Lutheran Church in 1987 for dealing with sexual misconduct. Another book, *Sex in the Parish*, by Karen Lebacqz and Ronald G. Barton, includes the guidelines developed by the North California Conference of the United Church of Christ. Many other judicatories now have policies that spell out the support that is available to alleged victims, alleged victimizers, and the congregation when there are charges of sexual misconduct.

With the assistance of legal counsel, most judicatories are better equipped to provide support to alleged victims than they are to the professional leaders about whom the allegations are made. Fortune, Lebacqz, and Barton agree that the issues of power that surround sexual impropriety are serious ones. The judicatory is rightly concerned about those who believe that they have been victimized by one who has been empowered as a professional leader. Were the judicatory to come down clearly on the side of the professional leader, that would only increase the sense of victimization of one who is already feeling overpowered.

On the other hand, not all allegations are true. When they are not, then it is the professional leader who feels victimized. Even if the allegations *are* true, the professional leader is still a person and a child of God, and there may be family members who also are bearing the burden of the charges, whether true or false.

In these days of increasing sensitivity and litigation in the area of sexual misconduct, it is wise for seminarians to review their judicatory guidelines for the procedures that are followed when charges are made and pay particular attention to any preventive suggestions. Fortune's book includes the ALC guidelines, with a section on Education and Prevention, an example of a synod policy for pastors, and also a section on Education and Support Opportunities, which focus on professional training, peer support, and consultation.

Lebacqz and Barton's book includes a chapter enitlted "The Bishop's Dilemma," which walks the reader through a sensitive and supportive judicatory response to a charge of sexual misconduct. More on preventive measures for judicatories is found in the UCC guidelines at the end of the book, specifically in a section of "Preventive Strategies for Church Members and Leaders."

Neither Jonathan nor Joan ever expect to find themselves in the middle of problems such as Fortune, Lebacqz, and Barton describe. Yet, either one of them could. The more done in the seminary to anticipate such potential problems and provide preventive education, the better prepared Joan and Jonathan will be for effective and faithful ministry. Again, this is an important area for those new to ministry and for those new to the judicatory. Knowing what to expect, knowing how the judicatory responds to such allegations, and knowing who to call at the first sign of difficulty is good supportive ministry.

There is no one type of person who is at-risk for sexual impropriety. There is no one personality, no one kind of life history, no one set of circumstances that inevitably spells trouble or immunity to it. Nevertheless there are some factors that can helpfully be kept in mind. Persons who feel good about themselves are less likely to need to feel good at the expense of others. Couples who have a healthy, loving, and mutually affirming relationship are less likely to look for appreciation elsewhere. Couples who nurture their spirituality and understand their relationship to be a significant expression of their spirituality are less vulnerable to breaking their covenant with each other. Professional leaders who feel valued by their judicatory will most often be loyal and will desire to be faithful as representatives of that religious body.

It is supportive and helpful preventive ministry for a judicatory to encourage Joan and Jonathan as new ministers to take care of themselves in healthy ways, to value themselves because God values them. Since Jonathan married after he entered congregational ministry the supportive circle needs to expand to include his wife.

Maintaining a vital marriage in combination with the open-endedness of parish ministry is not easy. Providing enrichment programs and opportunities for professional leaders and spouses to get away from time-to-time to renew their relationship is good ministry to ministers. The exclusion of marriage and family counseling from insurance coverage because of cost may be what Grandma used to call "penny wise and pound foolish." It would be interesting to know if a financial settlement in one major sexual misconduct lawsuit might not actually cost the judicatory more than the annual cost of coverage for marriage and family therapy for all the professional leaders in the judicatory. Would such coverage guarantee no sexual impropriety? Of course not. Those religious bodies that do provide such coverage still have situations of sexual misconduct. On the other hand, if even one such lawsuit was prevented because a professional leader was supported in attending to relational difficulties at home, would that not be good stewardship? Clearly so. In addition, the congregation would receive some of the benefits of a happier and healthier professional leader.

In the good times and in the bad, support is needed. By recognizing and valuing individual differences, support can be more individualized, more personal, and even more effective.

CHAPTER VI

Growth in Grace, Growth in Spirit

"We have this ministry" (II Cor. 4:1, KJV).

Ministry is not a personal possession, nor a personal right. It is a calling, a calling that comes to all persons and to professional leaders in a particular way. The call is to use our gifts to build up the community of faith.

But to say "We have this ministry" is different from saying *you* have a ministry, or *I* have a ministry. *"We* have this ministry," carries with it the understanding that ministry is not a personal, private, solitary calling. It is something that we have together. It is a mutual ministry.

A Ministry of Mutuality

The *Caring for the Caregiver* study found that many people were eager to talk about professional leadership support. Many of these persons were judicatory staff persons who were interested not only in telling what their religious body is doing to be supportive, but also in learning what other religious bodies are doing. That same level of interest was present at a conference in Wisconsin that addressed The Clergy Support Challenge of the 1990s. Many denominational staff persons and professional leadership support counselors came together to talk about what seems to help and what more needs to be done to be even more helpful to professional leaders; there was a strong theme of mutual ministry.

The theme of mutuality was also underscored by the repeated endorsement on the *Caring for the Caregiver* survey of congregational leader-lay support committees. Sometimes those committees do not fulfill their promise, which is one reason these committees need to clearly understand their purpose and limitations.

A wise professor of pastoral counseling, Dr. David Ostergren, pointed out that when caregiving is involved it is appropriate to question, "Whose need?" Whose needs are a mutual ministry committee to be meeting, and how can those needs best be met? If the professional leader looks to the committee for something the committee cannot give, then disappointment is inevitable. For the ministry to be mutual, the professional leader and the committee members must clarify and agree upon the committee's goals. The goals should be specific, realistic, attainable, and (if possible) measurable. Such an agreement makes staff support committees "user friendly," and it appropriates some of the best of goal attainment theory from the secular world.

But there is also a theological reason for moving in the direction of mutual ministry.

Growth in Grace

A theology of grace takes away the burden of having to measure up. That is a foreign concept to a society that, as Talcott Parsons said, is instrumental, activistic, and achievement-oriented. Within an achievement-oriented society, an individual has to measure up on his or her own. Self-esteem is based on self-assertion and success.

A theology of grace crosses out the "stars in my crown" way of thinking and offers in its place an invitation. Because all has been given, there is no need to strive to gain it all. We need only receive it. Because this is the day that the Lord has made, we do not need to make the day happen, we need only rejoice and be glad in it.

We are to rejoice together. God created us not for isolation, but for community. We are to rejoice and be glad in the day that the Lord has made, together. There is no Israelite apart from Israel. There is no Christian apart from the body of Christ, the communion of saints, the body of believers.

We are invited to open our hearts and receive the good things that the Lord gives to us. We also are invited to be followers of the way. It is not our way *to* the Lord. None is needed since God comes to us. Rather, we are invited to follow the way *of* the Lord.

The way of the Lord leads us to a recognition and appreciation of our mutual ministry, and so mutual ministry is growth in grace. For Christians, it means taking Ephesians 4 seriously as a guideline for ministry. Those gifted as pastors and teachers can equip the saints for the work of ministry, for the building up of the body of Christ. Professional leaders are gifted and called into ministry to equip ministers for their ministries, which builds up the body of believers.

Ministry is mutual ministry. What practical difference does this make to Joan or Jonathan? Plenty. Those who received their seminary educations years ago entered ministry as the minister. Ministry was what we did. Ministry is what we offered to others. Ministry is what they saw in us.

When Jonathan or Joan enter a ministry context not as *the* minister but as *a* minister called to equip others for *their* ministries, they foster a sense of mutuality. It also raises new reasons and possibilities for a mutual ministry committee.

One of those possibilities is that Jonathan might go about recommending members for the mutual ministry committee in a different way. Rather than as the minister who seeks others who will be supportive of his ministry, Jonathan would be looking for those who will help him discern the way his gifts can be used for equipping others for ministry. He will be seeking the kinds of resources he needs to help others to use their gifts for the common good (I Cor. 12). He becomes more effective in his role of supporting others for ministry. He also can let know what he needs from the congregation so he can offer more to them—time to breathe in as well as out, time away for reflection and renewed perspective, time for continuing education. Granted, this is a fairly subtle change in perspective, but it can produce significant results.

Joan might enter into a parish where the staff support committee has been working for some time and is very clear about how it needs to function. Before changing anything, Joan would be wise to study the current situation and its history. As she listens and works within the existing framework, Joan can keep in mind an understanding of herself as one called to equip others for their ministry and look for opportunities to channel some of the committee's energy in that direction.

Joan and Jonathan will have to remember that sometimes the language of "everybody a minister" is interpreted as the professional leader not wanting to do her or his job. The call to equip others for their ministry is no less encompassing, no less demanding, no less time consuming,

no less a pouring of oneself out in love and service than being *the*
minister. So the shifting of perception is not a shifting of work, but an
opening of a greater sense of appreciation for the vocation which all
share who accept the Lord's invitation to follow the way together.

Another Look at Church Growth

How do congregations and professional leaders grow?
   Together.
   The thesis of this book is that church growth and leadership support
are integrally related. This is true whether the direction of the growth is
in breadth of mission or depth of ministry. The spirituality of a community of believers is strengthened and deepened through mutual ministry,
since growth comes through caring and mission through ministry.
   Mistakenly, there are those who set ministry and mission against
each other, as if they are in competition, or as if one could happen without the other. That is not the biblical witness. Faithful ministry is the
result of mission and leads to mission. Faithful mission is the result of
ministry and leads to ministry. As is crucial for healthy life and for
balanced professional leadership, so with ministry and mission—breathing in and breathing out are not in opposition to each other. On the
contrary, each makes the other possible.
   Professional leadership support is a ministry of congregations and
judicatories that undergirds the ministry of professional leaders. Having
received ministry, the professional leader is strengthened to fulfill his or
her mission of equipping the saints for *their* work of ministry and mission. Congregational and denominational growth can happen in spite of
the professional leader, but is more likely to occur as a result of the
faithful ministry of a mission-minded leader. Caring for the caregiver is
a part of the rhythm of life, a deep, refreshing breath that leads to the
growth of the *person* in ministry and energizes the person in *ministry* for
reaching out to others. Therefore caring for the caregiver is truly a
growth model, both for professional leaders and for parishes, for ministry
and for mission.

The Caring for the Caregiver Survey

PROFESSIONAL LEADERSHIP SUPPORT SURVEY
Caring for the Caregiver Study
Gary L. Harbaugh, Ph.D., Project Director
Trinity Lutheran Seminary (614) 235-4136

The Caring for the Caregiver
study is being conducted with
a grant from the Lilly Endowment.

The following questions are designed to take a minimum of your time, but your responses will make a major difference in the accuracy and comprehensiveness of the *Caring for the Caregiver* study now under way with the support of the Lilly Endowment. The results are intended to provide a description of what is available for the support of professional leaders and their families in the various religious bodies.

Please check the appropriate answer and return the survey in the enclosed envelope. Please sign your response sheet and indicate whether or not you would be willing to be contacted by telephone for follow-up if needed.

If someone in addition to you, or in place of you, would be the most appropriate person to respond to the questions, please have that other person complete what you do not answer, or pass the form along.

It would help greatly if you could return the completed survey by the end of July, 1991. Thank you for your help. Please call if you have any questions. In appreciation for your time, each person who completes the survey and provides a mailing address will receive a summary of the survey results.

Your religious faith or denomination: _____

Coordination

1. At what levels does your religious body offer a coordinated support program for the personal care and counseling of professional leaders? (*Note: "personal care and counseling" means individual counseling or therapy, not peer support groups or continuing education alone;* please check all answers that apply).

    __National
    __Regional (*groupings* of dioceses, presbyteries, districts, etc.)
    __Single dioceses, presbyteries, districts, conferences, synods, etc.
    __None of the above

2. If your religious body permits the marriage of professional leaders, are the same counseling and therapy services available to *spouses and other family members?*

    __Yes __No

    __Yes, but with this difference

_____

_____

Coverage

3. If your religious body has a coordinated support program for the personal care and counseling (counseling or therapy) of professional leaders, is that care and counseling underwritten in whole or in part by an *insurance program?*

    __Yes, a commercial program
    __Yes, our religious body's self-insurance program
    __No

4. If your religious body has a coordinated support program for the personal care and counseling of professional leaders, approximately what percentage

of the *cost* of that care is borne *by the professional leader* (including insurance co-payments, if applicable)?

   ___   100% (professional leader pays all the cost)
   ___ 75-99%
   ___ 50-74%
   ___ 25-49%
   ___   1-24%
   ___   0% (no cost at all to the professional leader)

5. If the professional leader is married, what percentage of the cost of the care and counseling of *spouses and family members* is the responsibility of the professional leader (including insurance co-payments, if applicable)?

   ___   100% (professional leader pays all the cost)
   ___ 75-99%
   ___ 50-74%
   ___ 25-49%
   ___   1-24%
   ___   0% (no cost at all to the professional leader)
   ___ Not Applicable

Counselors

6. If your religious body has a coordinated support program for the personal care and counseling of professional leaders, and designated counselors are officially recognized and made available to provide those services, which of the following counseling disciplines are made available?

   ___Psychiatry
   ___Psychology (Ph.D., Psy.D, etc.)
   ___Psychology (Masters level)
   ___Social Work
   ___Career Counseling
   ___Pastoral Counseling (e.g., AAPC)
   ___Marriage and Family (e.g., AAMFT)
   ___Other _____

7. Are there national or regional standards (secular or ecclesiastical) that counselors must meet prior to being recognized by your religious body?

    __Yes __No   If yes, what are they?

_____

_____

Confidentiality

8. Whether or not your religious body has a *coordinated* support program for the care and counseling of professional leaders, is it possible for a professional leader to *independently and confidentially* seek out care and counseling from a private counselor?

    __Yes __No

If so, is the same available to a *spouse or family member*?

    __Yes __No

Comprehensiveness

9. If a private counselor is used for a problem that *meets the criteria* for a DSM-III-R (psychiatric) diagnosis, and the professional leader or family member is willing to file an insurance form or request financial assistance, is any of the cost of counseling covered by (Please check all that apply.)

    __Your religious body (national)?
    __Your religious body (regional)?
    __Your religious body (diocesan, presbytery, district, etc.)?
    __Insurance provided or sponsored by your religious body?
    __Other _____

10. If a private counselor is used for a problem that does *NOT* meet the criteria for a DSM-III-R (psychiatric) diagnosis, e.g., *marriage counseling*, and the professional leader or family member requests assistance, is any of the cost of counseling covered by (Please check all that apply.)

__Your religious body (national)?
__Your religious body (regional)?
__Your religious body (diocese, presbytery, district, etc.)?
__Insurance provided or sponsored by your religious body?
__Other_____

11. If a private counselor is used for *career/vocational counseling* and the professional leader or family member requests assistance, is any of the cost of counseling covered by (Please check all that apply.)

__Your religious body (national)?
__Your religious body (regional)?
__Your religious body (diocese, presbytery, district, etc.)?
__Insurance provided or sponsored by your religious body?
__Other _____

12. If some or all of the costs of private counseling are covered for the services of a private counselor, *which of the following counseling disciplines* does your religious body recognize as reimbursable providers of counseling services?

Disciplines	*Must they be supervised?*		*By Whom?*
__Licensed Psychiatrists	Yes	No	
__Lic. Psychologists (Doctoral)	Yes	No	
__Lic. Psychologists (Masters)	Yes	No	
__Licensed Social Workers	Yes	No	
__Other Licensed Counselors	Yes	No	
__Pastoral Counselors	Yes	No	
__Career Counselors	Yes	No	
__Marriage Counselors (AAMFT)	Yes	No	
__Other _____	Yes	No	

Counseling Specializations

13. Does your religious body have, or recommend, *specific* national or regional counseling programs for *specific difficulties* such as the following?

Yes   No   Name of counseling program

Divorce
Substance Abuse
Sexual Misconduct
Financial Impropriety
Career Development
Outplacement to Secular Work
Psychodiagnostic Assessment
Inpatient/Resident Care
Other_____

Concern and Concerns

14. If the judicatory head (Bishop, President, Presbyter, etc.) knows that a professional leader needs counseling and/or is open to receiving counseling, to what extent do you agree that the judicatory head should make *personal contact* with the professional leader to discuss any concerns the professional leader might have about the consequences of entering the counseling process?

Before the referral: *During treatment:*   *After treatment:*

_Strongly agree   _Strongly agree   _Strongly agree
_Agree   _Agree   _Agree
_Mildly agree   _Mildly agree   _Mildly agree
_Mildly disagree   _Mildly disagree   _Mildly disagree
_Disagree   _Disagree   _Disagree
_Strongly disagree   _Strongly disagree   _Strongly disagre

15. In the receptivity to personal counseling or other therapeutic treatment by a professional leader (and/or family member, if any), rank order from 1 to 5 the following "concerns" that professional leaders say they have. #1 = the *primary* concern; #5 = the *least* concern of the five that are listed:

_Confidentiality
_Financial feasibility
_Present job security
_Future vocational mobility
_Lack of good, available local resources

Choices

16. Different religious bodies seem to emphasize one of the following approaches to the care and counseling of professional leaders. Please identify which approach is closest to what your religious body typically provides by *(checking)* the description, then rank order the approaches based on your opinion (#1 = most desirable approach; #5 = least desirable approach).

(Check one)
___There is an identified religious body *staff person* who provides counseling services (may involve reporting to the judicatory)
___An identified religious body *staff person* provides confidential counseling (*no reporting* to the judicatory)
___An identified counselor (*not* a staff person) provides confidential counseling (*no reporting*)
___A counselor is chosen by the professional leader *from a list of "approved" counselors* who meet the religious body's standards for appropriate care (e.g., licensure, sensitivity to faith issues, etc.; *no reporting*)
___A counselor is chosen by the professional leader (*no list; no reporting*)

Please identify any other approach that you would have ranked #1 if it had appeared on this list: _____

Continuing Education

17. Some religious bodies supplement personal care through counseling and therapy with continuing education programs *designed* to *prevent* problems from reaching a crisis level. If your religious body does this, in which of the following areas are such preventive programs provided?

___Personal (stress management, physical and psychological self-care, etc.)
___Marriage (communication, balancing work and marriage, etc.)
___Family (children, family systems, etc.)
___Sexual Ethics in Ministry

_Chemical Health (addictions and co-dependency, etc.)
_Congregational (conflict management, leadership style, etc.)
_Congregational (team ministry, staff relations, etc.)
_Vocational (transition into or out of full-time ministry, etc.)
_Spiritual Growth
_Other _____

18. If your religious body (national, regional, or local) offers preventive continuing education programs, on the average how often would a professional leader have the opportunity to attend a program in one of the areas above?

_Once every two or more years
_Once a year
_More than once a year
_Preventive programs are not offered by our religious body

19. If your religious body offers preventive continuing education programs, how often would there be a program offered that a *spouse* could attend?

_Once every two or more years
_Once a year
_More than once a year
_Preventive programs which include spouses are not offered by our religious body

20. If your religious body (national, regional, or local) offers preventive continuing education programs, *when attendance is poor*, what would be the primary factors most professional leader would have for NOT attending? (Please check all that apply.)

_Distance (e.g., offered only regionally or nationally)
_Financial (e.g., costs too much)
_No awareness of a need for such programs
_Fear that attending will signal having a problem in that area
_Poor quality programs
_Other _____
_None: such programs in our religious body are always well attended

Care in Context

21. Some religious bodies encourage the development of peer support groups (parochial or ecumenical) and within the congregation professional-lay "mutual ministry" support committees. Your religious body recommends (please check all that apply):

_Parochial or denominational peer support groups
_Ecumenical peer support groups
_Congregational "mutual ministry" support committees
_Other_____
_None of these

22. If professional leaders in your religious body are encouraged to be involved in peer support groups or congregational "mutual ministry" committees, what do you think would be *major* factors involved in NOT attending a peer support group or in a professional leader's NOT establishing such a congregational committee? (Please check all that you think are MAJOR factors.)

_Time limitations
_No awareness of a need for such a group or committee
_Fear or distrust of sharing at a more personal level
_Need to maintain the appearance of everything going well
_Other_____

23. What forms of professional leadership support do you consider to be *essential* for a religious body to have in place if a professional leader is to feel supported by the religious body that leader represents? (Please check ONLY those that you consider to be *essential* for a religious body to offer.)

_Counseling or Therapy
_Preventive Continuing Education
_Peer Support Groups
_Congregational "mutual ministry" leader-layperson committees
_Other_____

24. If your religious body were able to substantially *increase* supportive services to professional leaders and, if any, their families, in which of the following areas do you think that additional support is most needed?

_Counseling or Therapy
_Preventive Continuing Education
_Peer Support Groups
_Congregational "mutual ministry" leader-layperson committees
_Other_____

25. Thank you very much for taking the time to complete this survey. Please complete these final questions. Then, in the space below, feel free to add any other information about the support of professional leaders which you believe is relevant.

Your name: _____

Are you willing to be contacted for follow-up?
     _Yes _No

If "yes," your telephone number: (_____) _____ - _____

The names of any others who could provide information concerning any of the above:
_____

Your religious body and mailing address:
_____
_____
_____
_____

Please address any correspondence to:

Gary L. Harbaugh, Ph.D.
Trinity Lutheran Seminary
2199 E. Main Street
Columbus, Ohio 43209

For Follow-Up

The following names and addresses are provided so that you might obtain additional information about the professional leadership support programs mentioned in the book. Some of the following are judicatory staff, some are caregivers in congregations or other ministry contexts. Both sources have provided insights and very helpful perspectives.

African Methodist Episcopal

Rev. Michael R. Bean
St. Paul AME Church
539 E. Long Street
Columbus, OH 43215
(614) 228-4113

Baptist

American Baptist

Dr. Craig Collemer
American Baptist Churches USA
P.O. Box 851
Valley Forge, PA 19482-0851
(215) 768-2000

Progressive National Baptist

Dr. Charles E. Booth
Mt. Olivet Baptist Church
2685 Halleck Drive
Columbus, OH 43209
(614) 231-5561

Southern Baptist

Dr. John Click
Immanuel Baptist Church
1415 S. Topeka Street
Wichita, KS 67211-3140
(316) 262-1452

Rev. Darrel E. Gabbard
Dublin Baptist
7195 Coffman Road
Dublin, OH 43017
(614) 889-2307

Dr. Ed Copeland
Director of Mission
Metro Columbus Baptist
    Association
4520 Josephus Lane
Columbus, OH 43227
(614) 238-0250

Dr. Orville Griffin
State Convention of Baptists
Baptist State Office
1680 E. Broad Street
Columbus, Oh 43202
(614) 258-8491

The Christian Church (Disciplies of Christ)

Trinity-Brazos Area
    of the Christian Church,
    Southwest
Ft. Worth, TX 76109
(817) 924-8793

Charles F. Kemp, Ph.D.
University Christian Church
2720 South University Drive
Fort Worth, TX 76109
(817) 926-6631

The Church of God

Jonne Crick, Office Coordinator
The Office of Ministerial Care
Keith at 25th N.W.
Cleveland, TN 37320-2430
(800) 762-5656

Eastern Orthodox Church

Fr. Frank A. Milanese
Greek Orthodox Cathedral,
    "The Annunciation"
555 N. High Street
Columbus, OH 43215
(614) 224-9020

Greek Orthodox Archdiocese of
    North and South America
Chancellor's Office
10 E. 79th Street
New York, NY 10021
(212) 570-3500

Holy Cross Orthodox School
    of Theology and
Department of Counseling and
    Spiritual Development
Fr. Nick Krommydas
50 Goddard Avenue
Brookline, MA 02146
(617) 731-3500

Eastern Orthodox Christian
    Church in America
Archbishop Michael and
    Fr. James
201 S. Hamilton Road
Columbus, OH 43213
(614) 238-0609

Episcopal

John Colon and Mary Japolo
Human Resources Program
815 Second Avenue South
New York, NY 10017
(212) 867-8400
(800) 334-7626

Rev. Chilton Knudsen
Diocese of Chicago
65 E. Huron
Chicago, IL 60611
(312) 751-4209

Reform Judaism

Rabbi Gary P. Zola, Ph.D.
Hebrew Union College-
    Jewish Institute of Religion
3101 Clifton Avenue
Cincinnati, Ohio 45220-2488
(513) 221-1875

Rabbi Joseph B. Glaser
Rabbi Elliot L. Stevens
Central Conference of
    American Rabbis
192 Lexington Avenue
New York, NY 10016
(212) 684-4990

Rabbi Jason Z. Edelstein
Coordinator of the National
    Conference of American
    Rabbis Hotline
Temple David
4415 Northern Pike
Monroeville, PA 15146
(412) 372-1200

Lutheran

**The Evangelical Lutheran Church
in America**

8765 W. Higgins Road
Chicago, IL 60631
(312) 380-2700

Office of Synodical Relations

Dr. Thomas Blevins

Division for Ministry

Dr. Joseph Wagner
Rev. Herb Carlmark
Dr. Phyllis Anderson
    Theological Education
Rev. A. Craig Settlage
    Candidacy
Madelyn Bussey
    Associates in Ministry
Dr. Paul Nelson
    Ministry Study
Dr. William C. Behrens
    Leadership Support
    ELCA Staff Support
    Committee Handbook and
    Pastoral Colleague Program
    (transition into ministry)
Dr. James Moy
    Inclusive Leadership
    Development
Rev. Serge Castigliano
    Specialized Pastoral Care
    and Clinical Education

Regional Pastoral Care Programs

Rev. Hermann Kuhlmann
6100 Channingway Blvd.
Suite 503
Columbus, OH 43232
(614) 759-9090

Dr. Gerald S. Troutman
1410 Ponce de Leon Ave., NE

Atlanta, GA 30307
(404) 371-9236

Rev. Asha George-Guiser
2707 Dorp Lane
Morristown, PA 19401
(215) 277-4459

Rev. Richard Vangerud
Rt. #3, Box 242V
Annandale, MN 55302
(612) 274-2365

Synodical Pastoral Care

Bishop Kenneth H. Sauer
Southern Ohio Synod
57 E. Main Street
Columbus, OH 43215
(614) 464-3532

Bishop Lavern G. Franzen
Pastor Susan Gamelin
Florida-Bahamas Synod
3838 W. Cypress Street
Tampa, FL 33607
(813) 876-7660

**The Lutheran Church –
Missouri Synod**

Bruce M. Hartung, Ph.D.
Office of Ministerial Health/
    Health and Healing
The Lutheran Church—
    Missouri Synod
1333 South Kirkwood Road
St. Louis, Missouri 63122-7295
(314) 965-9917

Mennonite

Rev. John A. Esau
General Conference Mennonite
    Church
Ministerial Leadership Services

722 Main Street
Box 347
Newton, KS 67114
(316) 283-5100

Methodist

Rev. Lynn M. Scott, Director
Division of Ordained Ministry
P.O. Box 871
1001 19th Avenue South
Nashville, TN 37202-0871
(615) 340-7389

Dr. John F. Few
St. John United Methodist
    Church
1800 Cypress Gardens Blvd., SE
Winter Haven, FL 33884
(813) 324-6347

Rev. George A. Buie III
Conway Methodist Church
3401 S. Conway Road
Orlando, FL 32812
(407) 277-5010

District Superintendent
    Dr. Dennis DeLacure
Florida Conference
    United Methodist Church
2125 E. South Street East
Orlando, FL 32803-6502
(407) 896-2230

The Presbyterian Church (USA)

Rev. R. Howard McCuen, Jr.
Associate for Services to
Committees on Ministry
Church Vocations
Ministry Unit
Presbyterian Church (USA)

100 Witherspoon Street,
Room M001
Louisville, Kentucky 40202-
    1396
(502) 569-5750

Dr. Rosalie Potter
Central Florida Presbytery
924 N. Magnolia Avenue
Suite 100
Orlando, FL 32803
(407) 422-7125

Rev. Paul E. Bodine
Milwaukee Presbytery
1933 W. Wisconsin Avenue
Milwaukee, WI 53233
(414) 931-7330

Rev. John N. Langfitt
John Knox Presbytery
1289 West Seminary Street
Richland Center, WI 53581-
    2098
(608) 647-8828

Sue Mooney, Vice Moderator
Scioto Valley Presbytery
6641 N. High Street
Worthington, OH 43085
(614) 847-0565

The Reformed Church in America

Rev. Alvin J. Poppen
Room 1808
475 Riverside Drive
New York, NY 10115
(212) 870-2958

Roman Catholic

Fr. Thomas Bevan
National Conference
   of Catholic Bishops
3211 Fourth Street, N.E.
Washington, DC 20017
(202) 541-3000

Brother Peter Fitzpatrick
National Organization for
   Continuing Education
   of Roman Catholic Clergy
   (NOCERCC)
1337 W. Ohio Street
Chicago, IL 60622
(312) 226-1890

Rev. Robert J. Wister
Executive Director,
   Seminary Department
National Catholic Educational
   Association
1077 30th Street, NW
Washington, DC 20007
(202) 337-6232

Fr. Emile Gentile, T.O.R.
Pastoral Ministry Secretary
Roman Catholic Diocese
   of Orlando
421 East Robinson Street
P.O. Box 1800
Orlando, FL 32802-1800
(407) 425-3556

APPENDIX III

Resources

During the study, the following resources currently utilized by different judicatories were among those who shared experiences.

Clergy Candidate Assessment Service

Dr. John E. Hinkle
412 W. Hintz Road
Arlington Heights, IL 60004-2439
(708) 577-5132

Dr. Hinkle provides interdenominational candidacy servicers and is a primary provider for the United Methodist Church.

Clergy Care

Kathleen Holimon, Administrative Secretary
Clergy Care
314 Highland Mall Blvd., Suite 110
Lutheran Social Services
Austin, TX 78752
(512) 454-4611

Counseling services developed by Dr. Peter Steinke are described in Chapter 3, Pan-Lutheran.

Consultation to Clergy

Dr. Eldon Olson
Pacific Northwest
766 B John Street
Seattle, WA 98109
(206) 937-3765

Consultation to Clergy is described in Chapter 3, Pan-Lutheran. Information was also provided by counselors Paul Stone, AAPC Diplomate and Supervisor, (206) 789-2366 and Larry Gaffin, Center for Life Decisions, (206) 325-9093.

Good Shepherd, Church Renewal Center

John "Fred" Lehr, Director
1006 South Sixth Street
Allentown, PA 18103
(1-800) 937-4903

Good Shepherd offers a hospital-related residential program for clergy and spouses and makes available a wide range of counseling and consultation services.

Halzeden

Chaplain Rock Stack
Box 11
Center City, MN 55012
(800) 257-7800

Kairos Care and Counseling^{SM}

Gary L. Harbaugh, Ph.D.
2601 Eagles Nest
Orlando, FL 32837
(407) 856-6204

Trinity Lutheran Seminary
2199 E. Main Street
Columbus, OH 43209
(614) 235-4136

Counseling services are described in Chapter 3, ELCA.

Dr. Charles Kemp
The Christian Church (Disciples of Christ)
2720 S. University Drive
Ft. Worth, TX 76109
(817) 926-6631

Dr. Kemp was one of the pioneers in concerns of the clergy and their care.

The Lilly Endowment

Dr. James Wind, Religion Division
The Lilly Endowment
P.O. Box 88068
Indianapolis, IN 46208-0068
(317) 921-7353

The Lilly Endowment has supported major projects of benefit to theological education. Additional information about those projects can be provided by Dr. Wind, Dr. Daniel Aleshire of the Association of Theological Schools in Pittsburgh, PA, (412) 788-6506, or Dr. Joseph O'Neill at Educational Testing Services in Princeton, NJ, (609) 734-5796.

Lutheran General Health System

Rev. Jerry Wagenknecht
Box 205
1775 Dempster Avenue
Park Ridge, IL 60068
(708) 698-8514

Menninger Foundation

Chaplain Peter Ross-Gotta
Box 829
Topeka, KS 66601-0829
(913) 273-7500, ext. 5622

Prairie View

Chaplain Tom Shane
1901 East First Street
Newton Falls, KS 67114
(316) 283-2400

Prairie View is one of the centers identified as a resource by the
Mennonite Church.

St. Barnabas Center

Mary E. Garke, Administrator
Dr. Don Hands, Clinical Director
St. Barnabas Center
Rogers Memorial Hospital
34700 Valley Road
Oconomowoc, WI 53006
(1-800) 767-1214

St. Barnabas Center offers six- to eight-week residential treatment programs, then aftercare at the three-, nine-, and eighteen-month anniver-
saries of discharge. A wide range of problems are treated, including substance abuse and sexual concerns, with specific attention given to
spirituality.

School of Professional Psychology

Dr. Russell Bent, Acting Dean
Wright State University

Dayton, OH 45435
(513) 873-3490

Former Dean Ronald E. Fox, Dr. Russell Bent, Dr. Allen Barclay, and
Dr. James Webb provided consultation in relation to research metho-
dology and clinical response to pastoral concerns.

Pastoral Care and Counseling - UMC

Dr. Don Houts
1701 S. Prospect, Suite 19
Champaign, IL 61820
(217) 356-4357

Counseling services described in Chapter 3, UMC.

Additional Resources

The Rev. Richard Vangerud
10572 116th Street, NW
Annandale, MN 55302
(612) 274-2365

Chaplain Mark Anderson
Ministerial Health Services
Fairview-Riverside Health Center
2450 Riverside Avenue
Minneapolis, MN 55454
(612) 371-6270

Sue M. Setzer, Associate Director
Career and Personal Counseling Service
4108 Park Road, Suite 200
Charlotte, NC 28209
(704) 523-7751

Dr. Harvey Huntley, Jr.
Career Crossroads

6900 Kingston Avenue
Knoxville, TN 37919
(615) 588-9753

Dr. Richard Hunt, Fuller Theological Seminary
Dr. Richard Murphy, Educational Testing Services
Dr. David Schuller, Association of Theological Schools
Dr. Murray Tieger, Reform Judaism

Church Career Development Council

The Association of Career Counseling Centers includes the following.
They are used by a number of religious bodies such as:

Adrian Dominican Sisters
American Baptist Churches, USA
Baptist General Conference
Church of the Brethren
Christian Church (Disciples of Christ)
Dominican Sisters
Episcopal Church
Evangelical Covenant
ELCA
General Conference Mennonite Church
Presbyterian Church (USA)
United Church of Christ
United Methodist Church

Rev. Jay Matthews, Associate Director
Midwest Career Counseling Center
2501 N. Star Road, Suite 200
Columbus, OH 43221
(614) 486-0469

Dr. John Davis
North Central Career Development Center
516 Mission House Lanem, NW
New Brighton, MN 55112
(612) 636-5120

Dr. Ronald Brushwyler
Midwest Career Development Service
P.O. Box 7249
1840 Westchester Blvd.
Westchester, IL 60154
(708) 343-6268

Rev. L. Guy Mehl
Lancaster Career Development Center
561 College Avenue
Lancaster, PA 17603
(717) 397-7451

Dr. Roy Lewis
Northeast Career Center
407 Nassau Street
Princeton, NJ 08540
(609) 924-9408

Dr. Harold Moore
Midwest Career Development Service
P.O. Box 2816
754 North 31st Street
Kansas City, KS 66110-0816
(913) 621-6348

Dr. Robert Urie
Career Development Center of the Southeast
531 Kirk Road
Decatur, GA 30030
(404) 371-0336

Rev. John Sims
Career and Personal Counseling Center
Eckerd College
St. Petersburg, FL 33733
(813) 864-8356

Dr. Robert Charpentier
The Center for Ministry
8393 Capwell Drive

Oakland, CA 94621-2123
(510) 635-4246

Dr. Elbert R. Patton
Career and Personal Counseling Service
St. Andrews Presbyterian College
Laurinburg, NC 28352
(919) 276-3162

Rev. William M. Gould, Jr.
Southwest Career Development Center
P.O. Box 5923
Arlington, TX 76005
(817) 640-5181

Dr. Stephen Ott
Center for Career Development and Ministry
70 Chase Street
Newton Centre, MA 02159
(617) 969-7750

Dr. Andrew Weaver
Pacific Center for Counseling and Career Development
537 South Commonwealth Ave.
Los Angeles, CA 90020
(213) 388-6711

Peggy Shriver
Church Career Development Council
Room 861
475 Riverside Drive
New York, NY 10115
(212) 870-2144

**Participant List
from the "Clergy Support Challenge of the 90's"
June 24-25, 1991
Milwaukee, WI**

Rev. Kelly W. Ackerman
Kansas East Conference, UMC
301 South National
Fort Scott, KS 66701

Terrence Baeder
Director Pastoral Care
Lutheran Social Services, IL
119 North Wyman Street
Rockford, IL 61101

Rev. Kelly B. Bender
Kansas East Conference, UMC
301 South National
Fort Scott, KS 66701

Rev. and Mrs. James Benes
Reformed Church in America
5129 West Beverly Avenue
Glendale, AZ 85306

Rev. Paul Bodine
Inter. Exec. Presbyt.
Presbytery of Milwaukee
1933 West Wisconsin Avenue
Milwaukee, WI 53233

Rev. Marvin Cheney
Christian Church/College Min.
302 South Main Street
Eurecka, IL 61530

Martha Coltvet
Interim Presby. Exec.
The Presbytery of North Waters
1401 Belknap Street
Superior, WI 54880-2705

Rev. and Mrs. Gerard DeLoof
Reformed Church in America
c/o R.R. 4, Box 40
Lennox, SD 57039

Mr. and Mrs. Frederick Dennard
Harlem Interfaith Counseling
215 West 125th Street, Lobby Floor
New York, NY 10027

Rev. and Mrs. Kenneth Dykstra
Reformed Church in America
c/o Rt. 1, Box 99
Pella, IA 50219

John A. Esau
Director, Min. Ldrshp. Ser.
Gen. Conf. Mennonite Church
722 Main Street
Box 347
Newton, KS 67114

Mary E. Garke, Administrator
St. Barnabas Center
Rogers Memorial Hospital
34700 Valley Road
Oconomowoc, WI 53006

Rev. Raymond Gau
Member Comm. Minist
The John Knox Presbytery
1289 West Seminary Street
Richland Center, WI 53581-2098

Richard V. Gilbertson
Assistant to Bishop
Northwest Synod, WELS
Box 730
Rice Lake, WI 54868

Gary L. Harbaugh, Ph.D.
Trinity Lutheran Seminary
2199 E. Main Street
Columbus, OH 43209

Dale Harner
Dist. Supt.
So. Indiana Conf., UMC
P.O. Box 5008
Bloomington, IN 47408

Robert G. Hudspeth
Pastoral Counselor
Interfaith Couns. & Trng. Serv.
401 East Main Street
P.O. Box 186
Kilgore, TX 75662

Rev. William Hurtig
Kansas East Conference, UMC
301 South National
Fort Scott, KS 66701

Rev. Robert J. Jacobs
Winnebago Presbytery
803 East College Avenue
Appleton, WI 54911

John Langfitt, Exec. Presbyter
The John Knox Presbytery
1289 West Seminary Street
Richland Center, WI 53581-2098

Rev. April Ulring Larson
Assistant to the Bishop
SE Minnesota Synod, ELCA
Assisi Heights
Box 4900
Rochester, MN 55903

Rev. and Mrs. Kenneth Leestma
Reformed Church in America
c/o 18800 Norwalk Blvd.
Artesia, CA 90701

John "Fred" Lehr, Director
Good Shepherd
1006 South Sixth Street
Allentown, PA 18103

Rev. R. H. McCuen
Presbyterian Church (USA)
100 Witherspoon Street, M001
Louisville, KY 40202

Mary Ann Moman
Chair, Bd. Ord. Minis.
So. Indiana Conf., UMC
P.O. Box 5008
Bloomington, IN 47408

Don Ott, Dist. Supt.
United Methodist Church/Milw.
1442 North Farwell Avenue,
Suite 508
Milwaukee, WI 53202-2900

Rev. Alvin J. Poppen
Reformed Church in America
475 Riverside Drive, 18th Floor
New York, NY 10115

Rev. Douglas Potter
Calvin Presbyterian
177 Glendale Drive
Long Lake, MN 55356

Susan Ruach, Conf. Staff
So. Indiana Conf., UMC
P.O. Box 5008
Bloomington, IN 47408-5008

Rev. Lynn M. Scott, Director
Division of Ordained Ministry
P.O. Box 871
1001 19th Ave. South
Nashville, TN 37202-0871

Rev. David Seip
Pastoral Counselor
17 Fountain Lake Court
Bloomington, IL 61704

Rev. and Mrs. Eugene Speckman
Reformed Church in America
c/o 76 Kendall Road
Kendall Park, NJ 08824

Rev. and Mrs. Louis Springsteen
Trinity Reformed Church
393 Old Tappan Road
Old Tappan, NJ 07675

Rev. Clarence Stangohr
LC-MS
1427 St. Clair Avenue
Sheboygan, WI 53081

Charlotte Still
Regional Associate
United Church of Christ
Office for church Life & Ldrship
700 Prospect Avenue East
Cleveland, OH 44115

Rev. and Mrs. Gordon Timmerman
Reformed Church in America
c/o 15802 Prospect Point Drive
Spring Lake, MI 49456

William Weber
Cons. to Pastors
St. Vincent Stress Center
8401 Harcourt Road
Indianapolis, IN 46260

Dr. Donald C. Houts, Presentation Leader
Dr. Gary L. Harbaugh, *Caring for the Caregiver* Study Review

Dr. James Sparks, Sponsor
Health and Human Issues
University of Wisconsin-Madison
610 Langdon Street, Room 314
Madison, WI 53703

Caring for the Caregiver Advisory Committee
Project support by The Lilly Endowment

Joseph O'Neill
Educational Testing Service
P.O. Box 24
Princeton, NJ 08542
(609) 734-5796

Craig Settlage
Division for Ministry
Evangelical Lutheran Church in America
8765 W. Higgins Road
Chicago, IL 60613
(312) 380-2700

Daniel Aleshire
Association of Theological Schools
10 Summit Park Drive
Pittsburgh, PA 15275
(412) 788-6506

James Wind
The Lilly Endowment
P.O. Box 88068
Indianapolis, IN 46208-0068

Criteria for Choosing a Counseling Resource

The following criteria for choosing a counseling resource are adapted from Gary L. Harbaugh, "When the Caregiver Needs Care,"*Lutheran Partners,* Evangelical Lutheran Church in America, September/October, 1991, pp. 11-17.

Since needs can be quite individual, are there any criteria that might be used to select one counselor or one program over another? In the past few years, there has been a proliferation of counselors and programs specializing in the needs of professional church leaders and their families. Here are some criteria that I would use if I were choosing a counseling resource:

1. History

One of the best predictors of future behavior is past behavior. Therefore I would lean toward those resource persons and programs that have been around for a while and have earned an excellent reputation. If a resource is not an individual but a program, then remember that the quality of the counseling program depends upon the individuals who provide services through the program. I would inquire carefully about the professional background and history of each of the individuals identified as program staff.

2. Experience in Ministry and with Ministers

For a parish pastor, an Associate in Ministry, or someone who works in a specialized ministry context, of particular importance is whether or not counseling resource persons can really understand what it is like to work within your ministry context. Have they had similar experience themselves? If they are of a different denominational background, or nondenominational, are they aware of the expectations of the judicatory within which you serve? The increasing popularity of "systems" approaches in counseling is a reminder that all of us live and work within family, community, and vocational systems that need to be considered when we really want to understand a situation.

3. Credentials

Because a person has certain letters after his or her name does not guarantee anything, but if I were concerned about a medical condition I would seek an M.D. or an R.N. rather than another M.Div.

With counseling resources, the situation is more complex. An M.D. is no longer necessarily the place to begin. What I would look for is a person educated and trained for the kind of service that I needed.

There are excellent counselors and therapists, psychologists and psychiatrists among them, but also other clinicians as well. Some states license Masters level counselors; some associations, such as the American Association of Pastoral Counselors, also certify counselors.

4. Competencies

Every licensed clinician can ethically counsel only within those areas in which that counselor has education and training. Were I looking for a counseling resource, I would look beyond credentials and licensing to those specific areas in which a potential counselor had particular competence. I might inquire about memberships and certifications in such professional associations as the American Association of Marriage and Family Therapists; the American Association of Sex Educators, Counselors, and Therapists; the American Association of Clinical Hypnosis; and, for vocational centers, the Church Career Development Council, etc. I would also not hesitate to ask a professional specifically about areas of special competency. No clinician that I know is equally competent in all areas of counseling. Were a counselor to be offended by my question about special competencies, presuming I had asked politely and with no hidden agenda, I would be inclined to seek services elsewhere.

5. Interests

While competent to provide services in a number of areas, counselors frequently have a special interest in a few of those areas. Where interests lie there is even more likelihood that a counselor will keep up with that interest through continuing education. Given the choice, I would prefer to have the counseling support of someone who is as well informed as possible in the area of my concern.

6. The Initial Consultation

It might seem strange that the initial consultation would appear under the heading of criteria for the selection of a counseling resource, but I believe that the selection process should not be completed until after you have an initial session with a potential counselor. You will notice that I have not listed the gender of the counselor or the counselor's age and race and similar variables as selection criteria. That is not because they are insignificant, but because for the most part they are not determinative of competent counseling. There are some exceptions to this, as for example when there are actual language barriers or cultural factors that will block communication. In those cases, however, a question to the counselor about competencies and interests can usually guide the selection.

On the other hand, what is determinative is whether or not you are comfortable with the counselor with whom you work. "Comfortable" in this sense means whether or not after talking with the counselor face-to-face you believe this person is someone you can trust and someone who you think is willing to make a real effort to understand you and the concerns that you have. If you do not trust the counselor or feel a lack of rapport, that does not mean the counselor is untrustworthy or someone who might not have excellent rapport with someone else, but that counselor is probably not the right one for you. If you are seeing the counselor for marital or family concerns, then how "comfortable" your spouse or family member is with the counselor is as important as your own impression.

7. Other Considerations

Some counselors are excellent at crisis intervention but are not as strong when it comes to ongoing counseling (which requires different skills for the beginning, middle, and ending phases). My own inclination is to agree at the first meeting that we'll look at the counseling relationship after three or four sessions to see whether or not it is "working." If not, perhaps a relatively minor mid-course adjustment is all that is needed. Or maybe it is time for a referral to another resource for a second opinion, or maybe another counselor would be better to undertake the next phase of the counseling. As a caregiver, what is most important to me is that the person who seeks help receives the help that the person needs. My concern is for the counselee, not that I be the one to provide the help. I'll refer if I think someone can get more of what they need elsewhere. I would hope that any counselor I would select would have the same commitment to my welfare.

Counseling as Growth in Spirituality

In *Pastor as Person* and in *God's Gifted People*, I suggested that a biblical understanding of personhood does not permit the splitting off of the spiritual from the physical, mental, emotional, and relational concerns of life. Unlike Western philosophy that separates mind and body (and spirit, if indeed there is any consideration of spirit), the Judeo-Christian perception of what it means to be human is holistic and integrative. This biblical perspective means that, rightly understood, to seek help for a medical problem or to seek counseling for a personal or relational or vocational problem is inherently and essentially an opportunity for spiritual growth and further integration as a person in Christ.

A biblical perspective also appreciates timely counseling, timely not only in the sense of chronological time but also in terms of "kairos" time —a time of God's inbreaking. For those who have eyes to see and ears to hear, counseling is a context within which the presence and power of the Holy Spirit is active, perhaps in a way that will change and transform life.

To think of counseling as a potential kairos time is to recognize that counseling is growth by the grace of God. We cannot create a kairos.

We can only be open to the possibility that God will use a particular crisis or turning point in our lives in a kairotic way, to help us appreciate even more the breadth and length and height and depth of the love of God in Christ Jesus.

When persons in ministry weary along the way, when the caregiver is in need of care, there is every biblical and theological reason to view that need not as a failure or a weakness, but as an opportunity for growth as a person and as a person in ministry. Opening ourselves as caregivers to our own need for care is itself a faithful response to God's grace. Colleagues in ministry can help each other by affirming and encouraging those who are being faithful by seeking help. Through such affirmation we further equip each other for the work of ministry, and so contribute to the building up of the Body of Christ.

BOOKS AND REFERENCES

Aleshire, Daniel O. *Faithcare*. Philadelphia: The Westminster Press, 1988.

Anderson, Dennis. "The Pastor as Parish Administrator." *The Many Faces of Pastoral Ministry*, Herbet W. Chilstrom and Lowell G. Almen, eds. Minneapolis: Augsburg Publishing House, 1989.

Anderson, Herbert. *The Family and Pastoral Care*. Philadelphia: Fortress Press, 1984.

Barnhouse, Ruth Tiffany. *Clergy and the Sexual Revolution*. Washington, DC: The Alban Institute, 1978.

Bope, E.T., R. M. Casto, G. L. Harbaugh, T. S. Jost, M. Julia, D. B. Lee, L. Platt, A. Thompson, W. R. Waugaman, and P. T. Williams. *Interprofessional Care and Collaborative Practice*. Pacific Grove, CA: Brooks/Cole Publishing Co., 199-.

Bowen, Murray. *Family Therapy in Clinical Practice*. New York: Jason Aranson, 1978.

Byers, Sandra R., Robert T. McLaughlin, and R. Michael Casto, eds. "The Five A's of Health Care Quality: An Interprofessional Perspective on Health Care Cost Containment." *Interprofessional Education and Practice Occasional Papers*, Number 4 (1990). Columbus, OH: The Health Care Cost Containment Public Policy Panel and the Commission on Interprofessional Education and Practice.

Childs, Jr., James M. *Faith, Formation, and Decision*. Minneapolis: Fortress Press, 1992.

Chilstrom, Herbert W., and Lowell G. Almen, eds. *The Many Faces of Pastoral Ministry*. Minneapolis: Augsburg Publishing House, 1989.

Clinebell, Howard J. Jr., and Charlotte H. Clinebell. *The Intimate Marriage.* New York: Harper & Row, 1970.

Coger, Marian. *Women in Parish Ministry: Stress and Support.* Washington, DC: The Alban Institute, 1985.

Deming, L., and J. Stubbs. *Men Married to Ministers.* Washington, DC: The Alban Institute, 1986.

Elhard, Leland E. "Narcissism and the Relation Between Pastor and Congregation." *Trinity Review,* 14:1, Spring, 1992.

Faul, John, and David Augsburger. *Beyond Assertiveness.* Waco, TX: Calibre Books, 1980.

Fortune, Marie. *Is Nothing Sacred? When Sex Invades the Pastoral Relationship.* New York: HarperCollings, 1989.

Friedman, Edwin H. *Generation to Generation: Family Process in Church and Synagogue.* New York: Guilford Publications, 1986.

Gilbert, Barbara G. *Who Ministers to Ministers? A Study of Support Systems for Clergy and Spouses.* Washington, DC: The Alban Institute, 1987.

Grant, Brian. *Reclaiming the Dream: Marriage Counseling in the Parish Context.* Nashville: Abingdon Press, 1986.

Hahn, Celia A., ed. *Especially for Women.* Washington, DC: The Alban Institute, 1992.

Hahn, Celia A. *Sexual Paradox: Creative Tensions in Our Lives and Our Congregations.* New York: Pilgrim Press, 1991.

Hahn, Celia A., ed. *What Makes Churches Grow? The Best of Action Information.* Washington, DC: The Alban Institute.

Harbaugh, Gary L. *God's Gifted People.* Minneapolis: Augsburg Publishing House, 1988, Expanded Edition, 1990.

___*Pastor as Person.* Minneapolis: Augsburg Publishing House, 1984.

___"Pace in Learning and Life: Prelude to Pastoral Burnout." *Seminary and Congregation: Integrating Learning, Ministry, and Mission.* Association of Professional Education for Ministry, LeRoy Aden, ed. (1983).

___"Pastoral Burnout: A View from the Seminary," with Evan Rogers, Statistician. *Journal of Pastoral Care.* Vol. 38, No.2, 1984.

___"The Pastor's Spouse," with William C. Behrens. *Trinity Review.* Columbus, OH, Fall, 1984.

___"Personhood of Pastor, Significance of," in *Dictionary of Pastoral*

Care. Rodney J. Hunter, ed. Nashville: Abingdon Press, 1990, 910-911.

___"The Person in Ministry." *Trinity Review* (Spring, 1983). Columbus, OH.

___"The Person in Ministry: Personality Type and the Seminary." *Research in Psychological Type* (1984). Mississippi State University.

___*The Faith-hardy Christian*. Minneapolis: Augsburg Publishing House, 1986.

___"When the Caregiver Needs Care," *Lutheran Partners* (August-September, 1991). Chicago: Division for Ministry, ELCA.

Harbaugh, Gary L., William C. Behrens., Jill M. Hudson., and Roy M. Oswald. *Beyond the Boundary: Meeting the Challenge of the First Years of Ministry*. Washington, DC: The Alban Institute, 1986.

Harbaugh, Gary L., and Marlene E. Harbaugh. "You Don't Have To Be Lonely." *Partnership* (May-June, 1985).

Harbaugh, Gary L., with Lewis Tagliaferre. *Recovery from Loss*. Deerfield Beach, FL: Health Communications, Inc., 1990.

Haugk, Kenneth C. *Antagonists in the Church: How to Identify and Deal with Destructive Conflict*. Minneapolis: Augsburg Publishing House, 1988.

Hirsch, Sandra, and Jean Kummerow. *LifeTypes*. New York: Warner Books, 1989.

Houts, Donald C. "Pastoral Care for Pastors," *Psychology Today* 25:3 (1977): 186-96.

___"Pastoral Care of Pastors." *Dictionary of Pastoral Care*. Rodney J. Hunter, ed., Nashville, Abingdon Press, 1990.

Hulme, William. *Managing Stress in Ministry*. San Franscisco: Harper, 1985.

Hulme, William and Lucy Hulme. *Practicing Marriage*. Minneapolis: Augsburg Publishing House, 1987.

Hunt, Harley, ed. *The Stained Glass Fishbowl: Strengthening Clergy Marriages*. Valley Forge, PA: Ministers Council, American Baptist Churches, 1990.

Hunt, Richard A., John E. Hinkle, and H. Newton Maloney. *Clergy Assessment and Career Development*. Nashville: Abingdon, 1990.

Hunter, Rodney J., ed. *Dictionary of Pastoral Care*. Nashville: Abingdon Press, 1990. cf. especially pp. 883-911.

Keller, John. *Let Go, Let God.* Minneapolis: Augsburg Publishing House, 1985.

Kemp, Charles. *The Caring Pastor.* Nashville: Abingdon, 1985.

Kerr, Michael E. "Chronic Anxiety and Defining a Self." *Atlantic Monthly* (September, 1988).

Kerr, Michael E., and Murray Bowen. *Family Evaluation: An Approach Based on Bowen Theory.* New York: Norton, 1988.

Lange, Arthur J., and Patricia Jakubowski. *Responsible Assertive Behavior.* Champaign, IL: Research Press, 1976.

Leas, Speed B. *Should the Pastor Be Fired? How to Deal Constrctively with Clergy-Lay Conflict.* Washington, DC: The Alban Institute, 1980.

Lebacqz, Karen, and Ronald C. Barton. *Sex in the Parish.* Louisville: Westminster/John Knox, 1991.

Lester, Andrew D. *Coping with Your Anger: A Christian Guide.* Philadelphia: Westminster, 1983.

Mace, David, and Vera. *What's Happening to Clergy Marriages.* Nashville: Abingdon, 1980.

Mead, Loren B., Barry H. Evans, E. W. Mills, and Clement. W. Welsh. *Personal and Professional Needs of the Clergy of the Episcopal Church.* Washington, DC: The Alban Institute, 1988.

Moremen, William M. *Developing Spiritually and Professionally.* Philadelphia: Westminster 1984.

Nuechterlein, Anne Marie. *Improving Your Multiple Staff Ministry: How to Work Together More Effectively.* Minneapolis: Augsburg Press, 1989.

Neuchterlein, Anne M., and Celia A. Hahn. *The Male-Female Church Staff: Celebrating the Gifts, Confronting the Challenges.* Washington, DC: The Alban Institute, 1990.

Oates, Wayne. *The Minister's Own Mental Health.* Great Neck, NY: Channel Press, 1955.

Oden, Thomas. *Becoming a Minister.* New York: Crossroad, 1987.

O'Neill, Joseph P. *Ministry Research Notes.* Educational Testing Service, Princeton, NJ. See Jerilee Grandy and Mark Greiner, "Academic Preparation of Master of Divinity Candidates," Fall, 1990, and Joseph P. O'Neill, and Richard T. Murphy, "Changing Age and Gender Profiles Among Entering Seminary Students," Spring, 1991.

Oswald, Roy M. *Clergy Self-Care: Finding a Balance for Effective*

Ministry. Washington, DC: The Alban Institute, 1991.

___*Crossing the Boundary Between Seminary and Parish.* Washington, DC: The Alban Institute, 1979.

___*How to Build a Support System for Your Ministry.* Washington, DC: The Alban Institute, 1991.

___*New Beginnings: The Pastorate Start-up Workbook.* Washington, DC: The Alban Institute, 1977.

___*The Pastor as Newcomer.* Washington, DC: The Alban Institute, 1977.

___*Running Through the Thistles: Terminating a Ministerial Relationship with a Parish.* Washington, DC: The Alban Institute, 1978

___*Severely Isolated Clergy.* Washington, DC: The Alban Institute, 1981.

Oswald, Roy M., C. T. Gutierrez, and L. S. Dean. *Married to the Minister.* Washington, DC: The Alban Institute, 1980.

Oswald, Roy M., Gail Hinand, William Chris Hobgood, and Barton Lloyd. *New Visions for the Long Pastorate.* Washington, DC: The Alban Institute, 1983.

Oswald, Roy M., and Otto Kroeger. *Personality Type and Religious Leadership.* Washington, DC: The Alban Institute, 1988.

Patton, John. "The Pastoral Care of Pastors," *The Christian Ministry*, 11:4 (1980): 832.

Patton, John, and Brian Child. *Christian Marriage and Family.* Nashville: Abingdon, 1988.

Pierce, Carol, and Bill Page. *The Male-Famale Continuum: Paths to Colleagueship.* Laconia, NH: New Dynamics, 1986.

Provost, Judy. *Work, Play and Type: Achieving Balance in Your Life.* San Francisco: Consulting Psychologists Press, 1990.

Randall, Robert. *The Eternal Triangle: Pastor, Spouse, and Congregation.* Minneapolis: Fortress, 1992.

___"Ministers and Churches at Risk." *The Christian Century* (November 20-27, 1991).

___*Pastor and Parish: The Psychological Core of Ecclesiastical Conflicts.* New York: Human Sciences Press, 1988.

___*Putting the Pieces Together: The Guidance of a Pastoral Psychologist.* New York: Pilgrim Press, 1986.

Rassieur, Charles R. "Career Burnout Prevention Among Pastoral Counselors and Pastors," in Stone and Clements, *Handbook for*

Basic Types of Pastoral Care and Counseling. Nashville: Abingdon Press, 1991.

___*Stress Management for Ministers.* Philadelphia: Westminster, 1982.

Rediger, G. Lloyd. *Coping with Clergy Burnout.* Valley Forge: Judson Press, 1982.

___*Ministry and Sexuality: Cases, Counseling, and Care.* Minneapolis: Augsburg, 1990.

Rutter, Peter. *Sex in the Forbidden Zone.* Los Angeles: Jeremy P. Tarcher, 1989.

Sager, Allan. *Gospel Centered Spirituality.* Minneapolis: Augsburg, 1990.

Sauer, Kennth H. "The Pastor as Parish Theologian." *The Many Faces of Pastoral Ministry,* Herbert W. Chilstrom and Lowell G. Almen. Minneapolis: Augsburg, 1989.

Schaper, Donna. *Common Sense about Men and Women in the Ministry* Washington, DC: The Alban Institute, 1990.

Schuller, David S., Merton Strommen, and Milo Brekke, eds. *Ministry in America.* New York: Harper & Row, 1980.

Steinke, Peter. *How Your Church Family Really Works.* Washington, DC: The Alban Institute, in publication.

___"How Your Church Family Works," "The Congregation as an Emotional System," "Murmuring," "Without a Vision, the Leader Perishes," in *New Creation*, published by Peter Steinke. See Appendix III.

Stone, Howard. *The Caring Church.* San Francisco: Harper & Row, 1983.

Stone, Howard, and William M. Clements, eds., *Handbook for Basic Types of Pastoral Care and Counseling.* Nashville: Abingdon Press, 1991.

Tagliaferre, Lewis, and Gary L. Harbaugh. *Recovery from Loss.* Deerfield Beach, FL: Health Communications, Inc., 1990.

Taylor, Walter F., Jr., "I Timothy 3:1-7: The Public Side of Ministry." *Trinity Review* 14:1 (Spring, 1992).

Tournier, Paul. *The Meaning of Persons.* New York: Harper & Bros., 1957.

von Lackum, N.J., and J. P. von Lackum III. *Clergy Couples.* Washington, DC: The Alban Institute, 1979.

Wegscheider, Sharon. *Another Chance: Hope and Health for the Alcoholic Family.* Palo Alto: Science and Behavior Books, 1981.

Woititz, Janet. *Adult Children of Alcoholics*, expanded edition.

DeerfieldBeach, FL: Health Communications, Inc., 1990.
Whybrew, Lyndon E. *Minister, Wife, and Church: Unlocking the
Triangle.* Washington, DC: The Alban Institute, 1984.

The Alban Institute:
an invitation to membership

The Alban Institute, begun in 1979, believes that the congregation is essential to the task of equipping the people of God to minister in the church and the world. A multi-denominational membership organization, the Institute provides on-site training, educational programs, consulting, research, and publishing for hundreds of churches across the country.

The Alban Institute invites you to be a member of this partnership of laity, clergy, and executives—a partnership that brings together people who are raising important questions about congregational life and people who are trying new solutions, making new discoveries, finding a new way of getting clear about the task of ministry. The Institute exists to provide you with the kinds of information and resources you need to support your ministries.

Join us now and enjoy these benefits:

CONGREGATIONS, The Alban Journal, a highly respected journal published six times a year, to keep you up to date on current issues and trends.

Inside Information, Alban's quarterly newsletter, keeps you informed about research and other happenings around Alban. Available to members only.

Publications Discounts:

☐ 15% for Individual, Retired Clergy, and Seminarian Members
☐ 25% for Congregational Members
☐ 40% for Judicatory and Seminary Executive Members

Discounts on Training and Education Events

Write our Membership Department at the address below or call us at (202) 244-7320 for more information about how to join The Alban Institute's growing membership, particularly about Congregational Membership in which 12 designated persons receive all benefits of membership.

The Alban Institute, Inc.
4125 Nebraska Avenue, NW
Washington, DC 20016